Wings
A Tribute to Kahlil Gibran

by

Karen Haughey

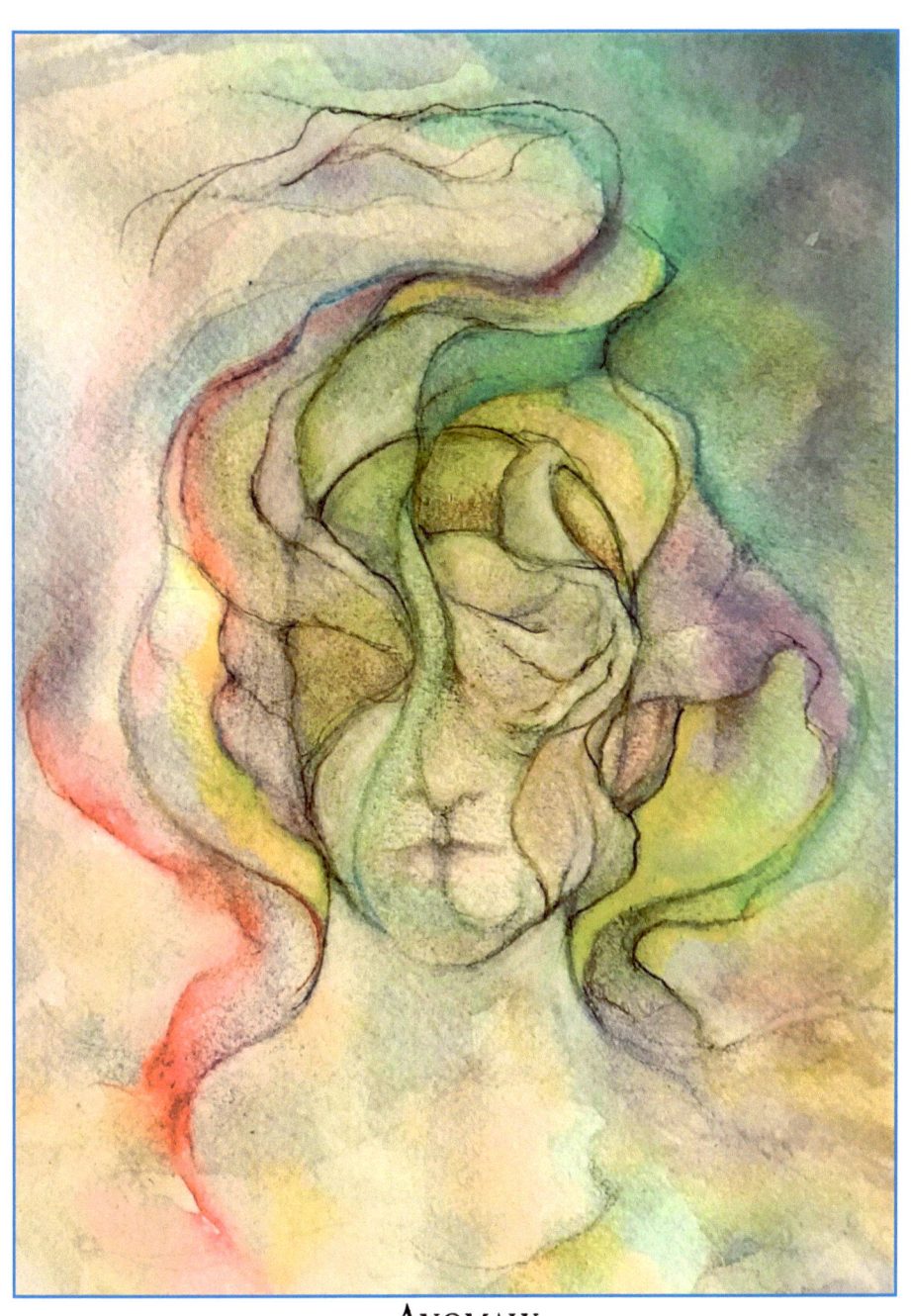

ANOMALY

ISBN: 978-1-952194-27-6

Quotes from *The Prophet* and *Sand and Foam* by Kahlil Gibran

Cover & Interior Art: All images copyright © 2023 by Karen Haughey

Front Cover Art: "Anomale"
Back Cover Art: "The Elements"

Book interior and cover design by Melanie Gendron

First Edition 2023

Printed in the United States of America

Available from:
RiverSanctuaryPublishing.com
Amazon.com

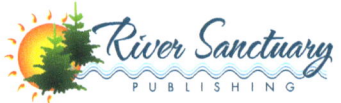

River Sanctuary Publishing
P.O. Box 1561
Felton, CA 95018
www.riversanctuarypublishing.com

Dedicated to the awakening of the New Earth

Wings
A Tribute to Kahlil Gibran

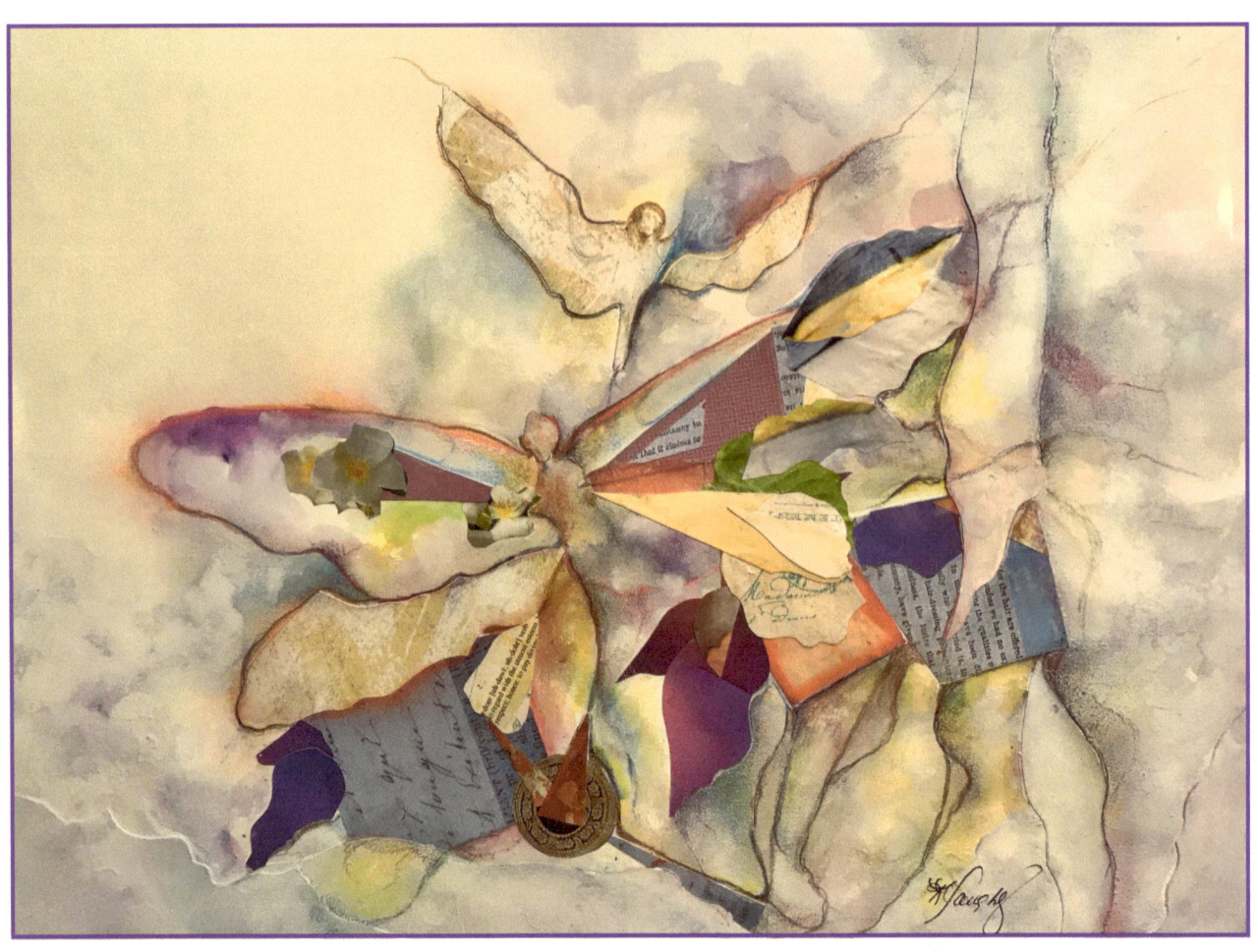

FLIGHT

Preface

Kahlil Gibran was born in 1883 in Lebanon, and passed away in 1931 at the age of 41 in New York City. He was a philosopher, author, and artist that gifted spiritual inspiration by expressing his personal visions through his magnificent art.

His books contained a great reservoir of intelligence, insight, intuitive cognition, and beauty, while celebrating the meaning of life that most seem to overlook in everyday society.

One of his most familiar books, *The Prophet*, was published in 1923, and has been translated into more than 100 languages.

One of my personal favorites, *Sand and Foam*, is a book of aphorisms, written by Gibran in 1926.

Some of his original artwork is placed within the archives of the Metropolitan Museum of Art in New York City, which I had the great honor of viewing in 1991.

If I had the ability to travel backward in time, he would be the one person with whom I would have loved to have a conversation.

Karen Haughey
Fremont, California
02/2023

Contents

*Art is one step from
the visibly known
to the unknown.*

–Kahlil Gibran

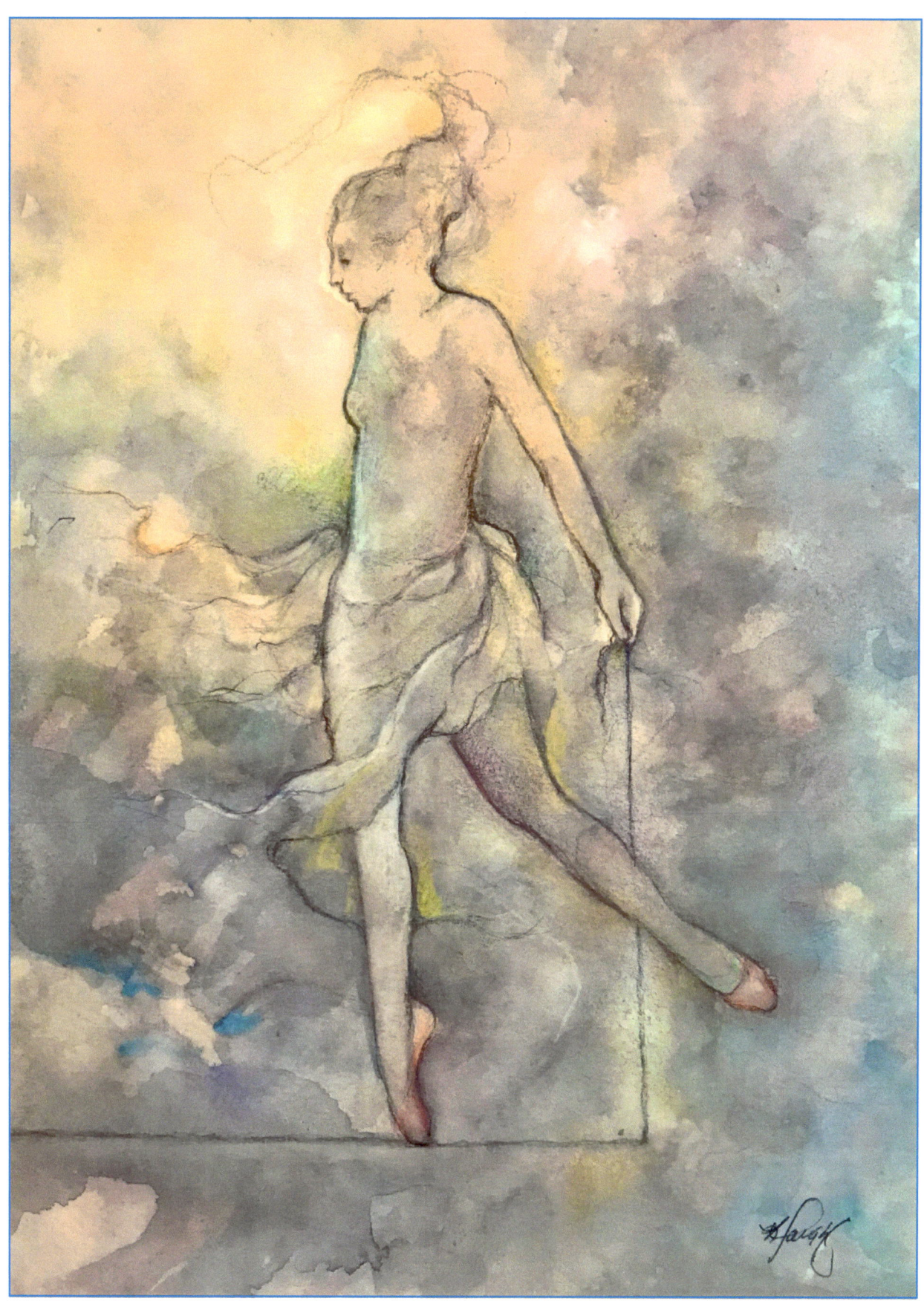

The Aerialist

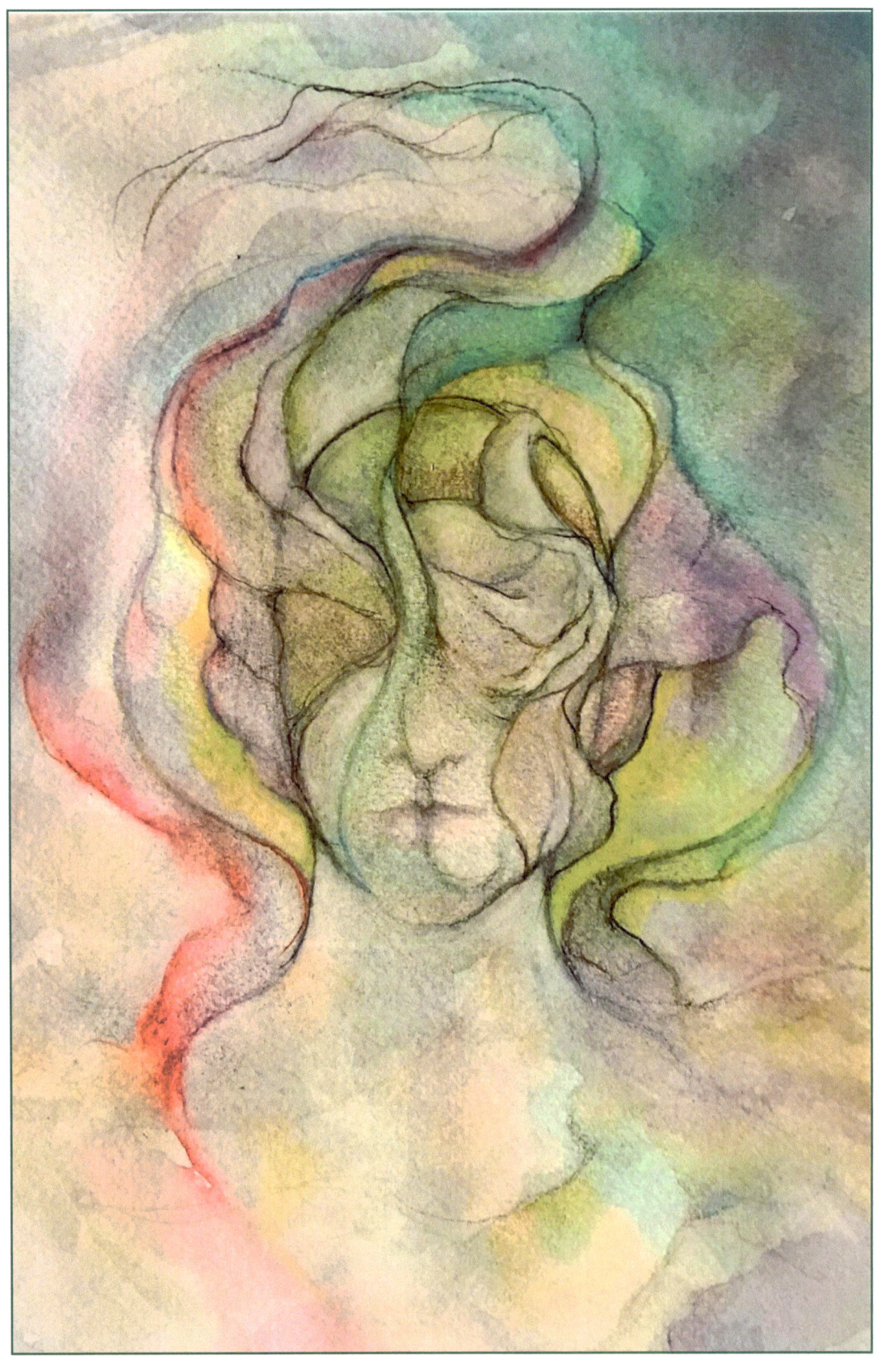

ANOMALY

The subtlest beauty in our lives is unseen or unheard.

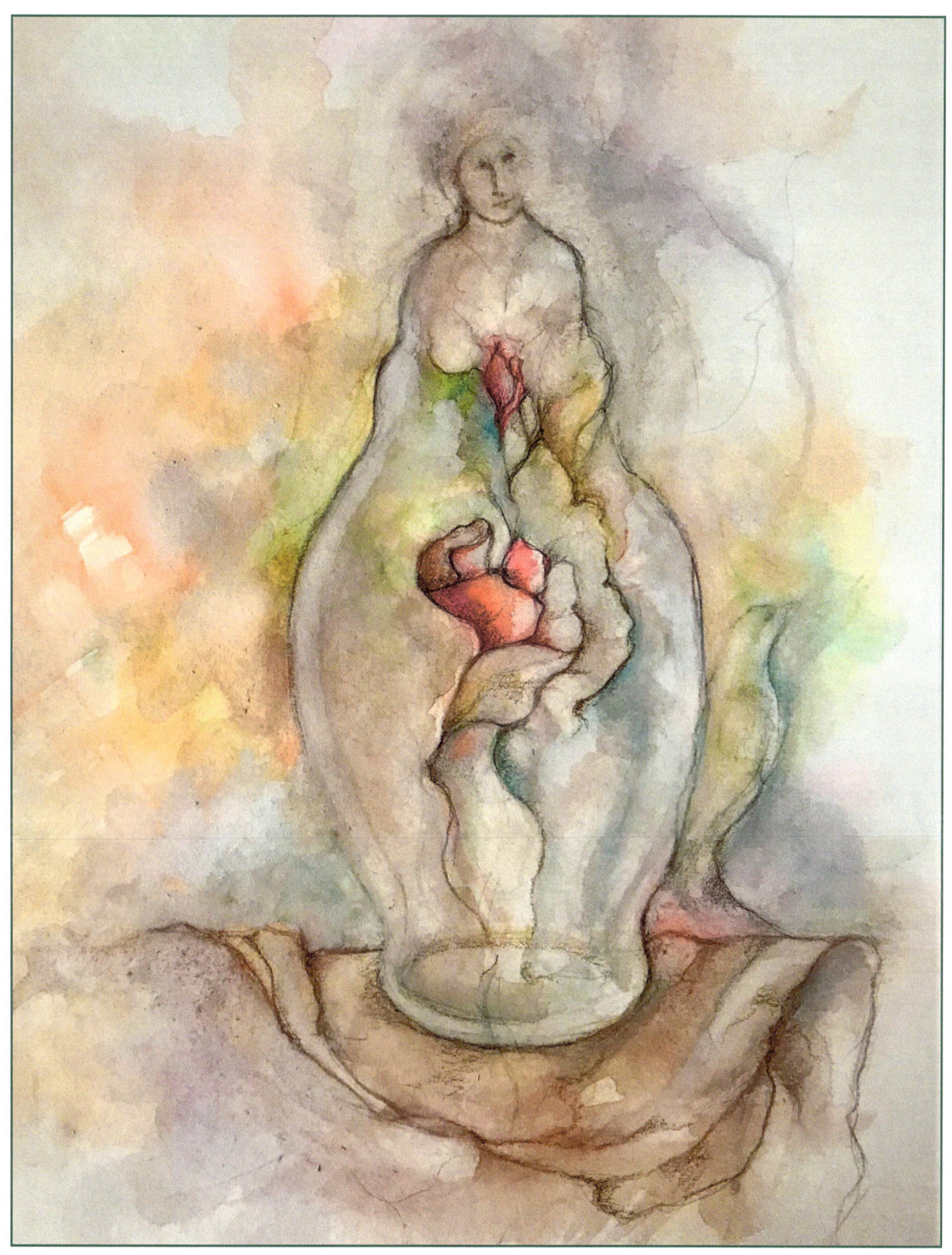

BUD VASE

A pearl is a temple built by pain around a grain of sand.
What longing built our bodies and around what grains?

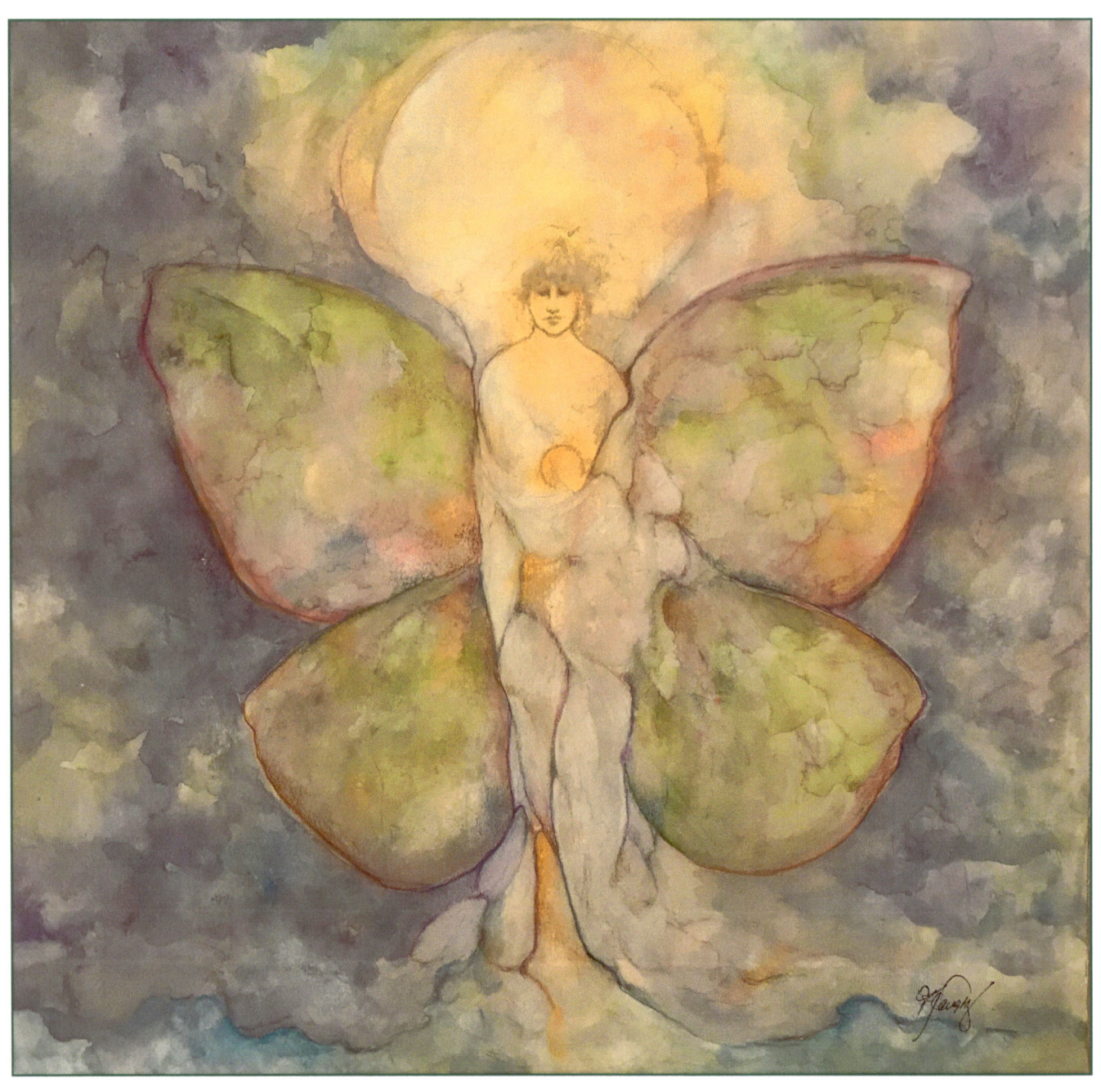

Cocoon

Inspiration will always sing,
Inspiration will never explain.

THE ELEMENTS

The deep and the high go to the depth,
or to the height in a straight line;
only the spacious can move in circles.

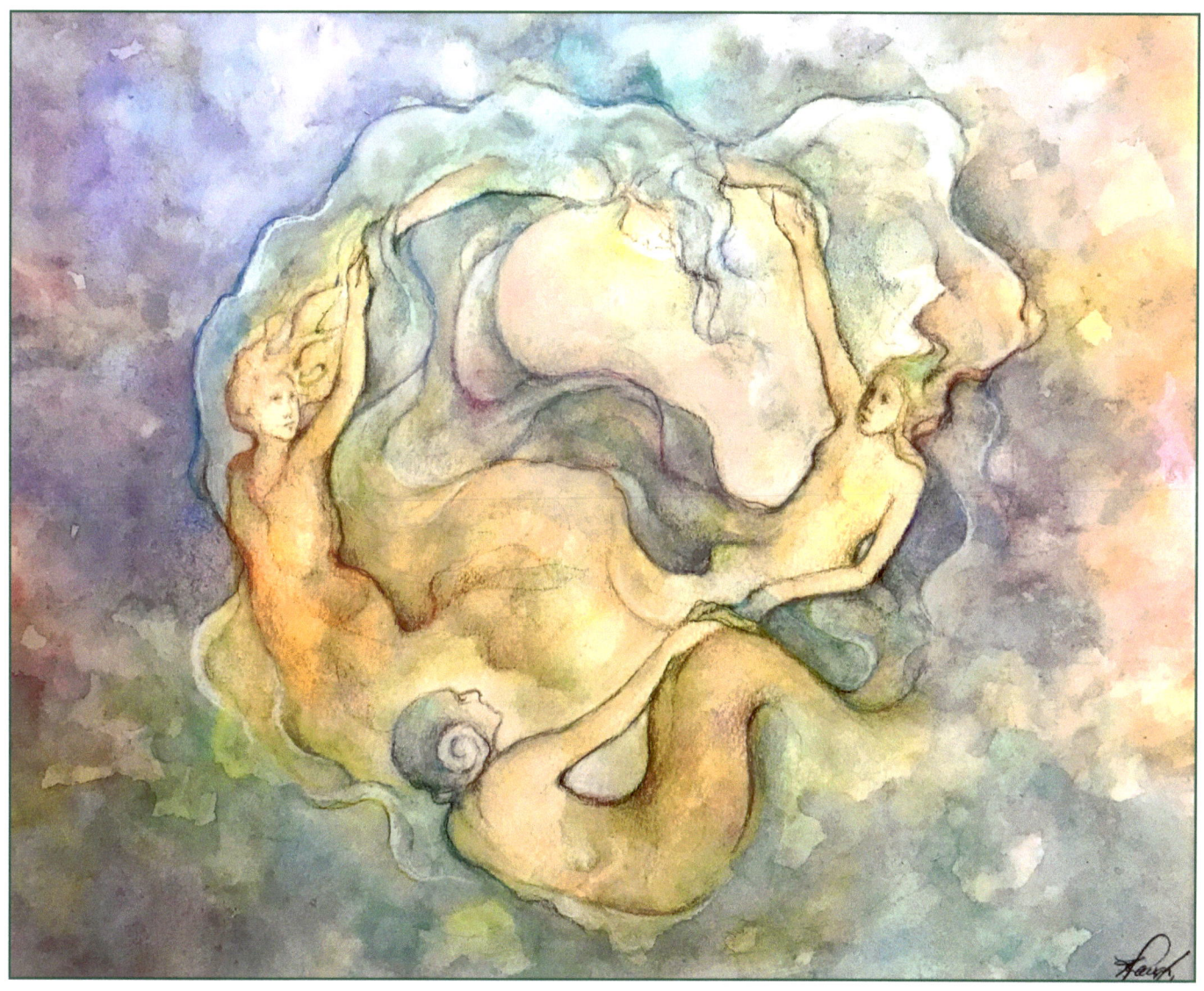

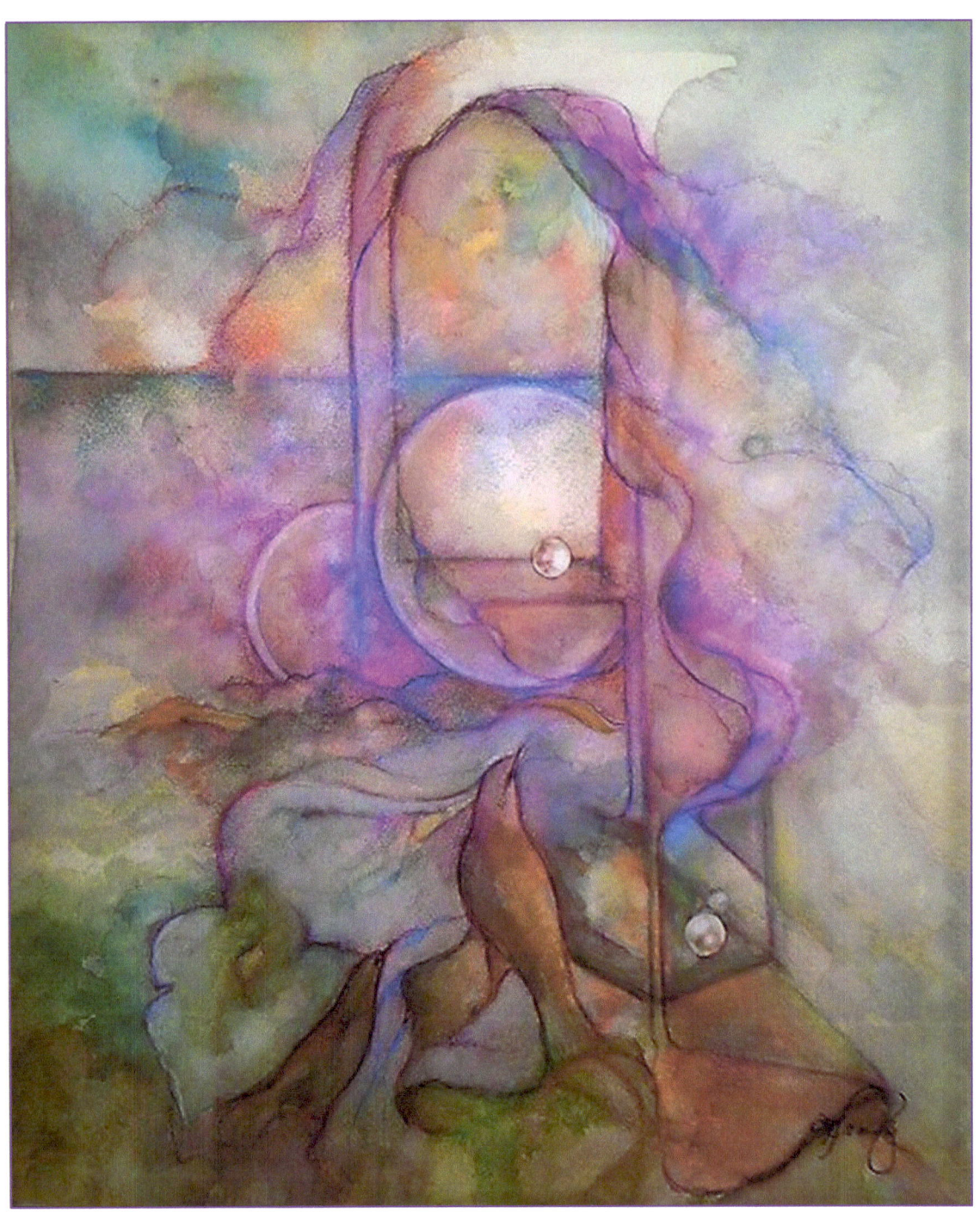

EARTH AND SEA

I am forever walking upon these shores
betwixt the sand and foam.
The high tide will erase my foot prints,
and the wind will blow away the foam.

But the sea and the shore
will remain forever.

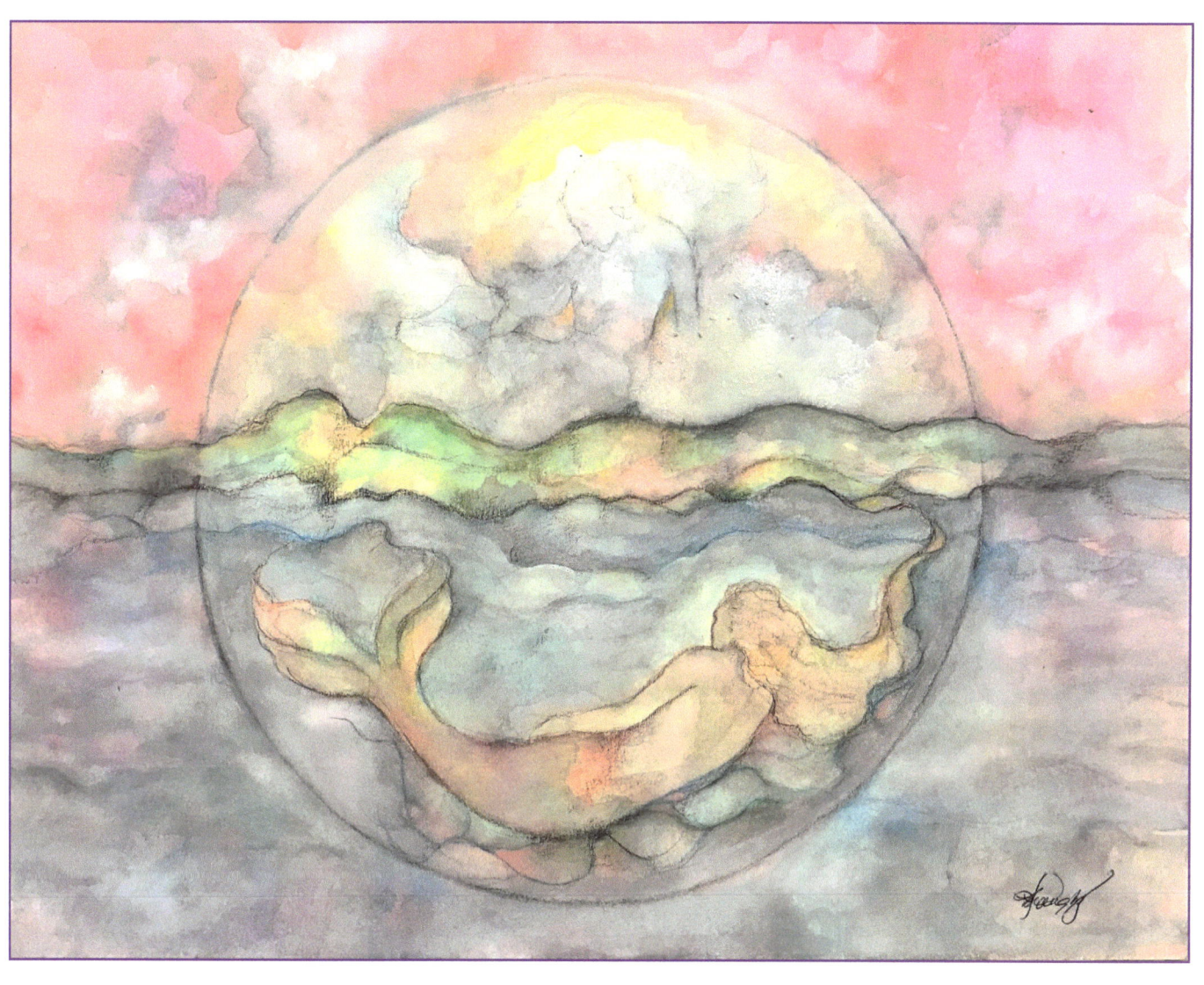

EARTH PORTRAIT

They say to me in their awakening,
you and the world you live in
are but a grain of sand
upon the infinite shore
of an infinite sea.
And in my dream
I say to them,
I am the infinite sea,
and all worlds are
but grains of sand
upon my shore.

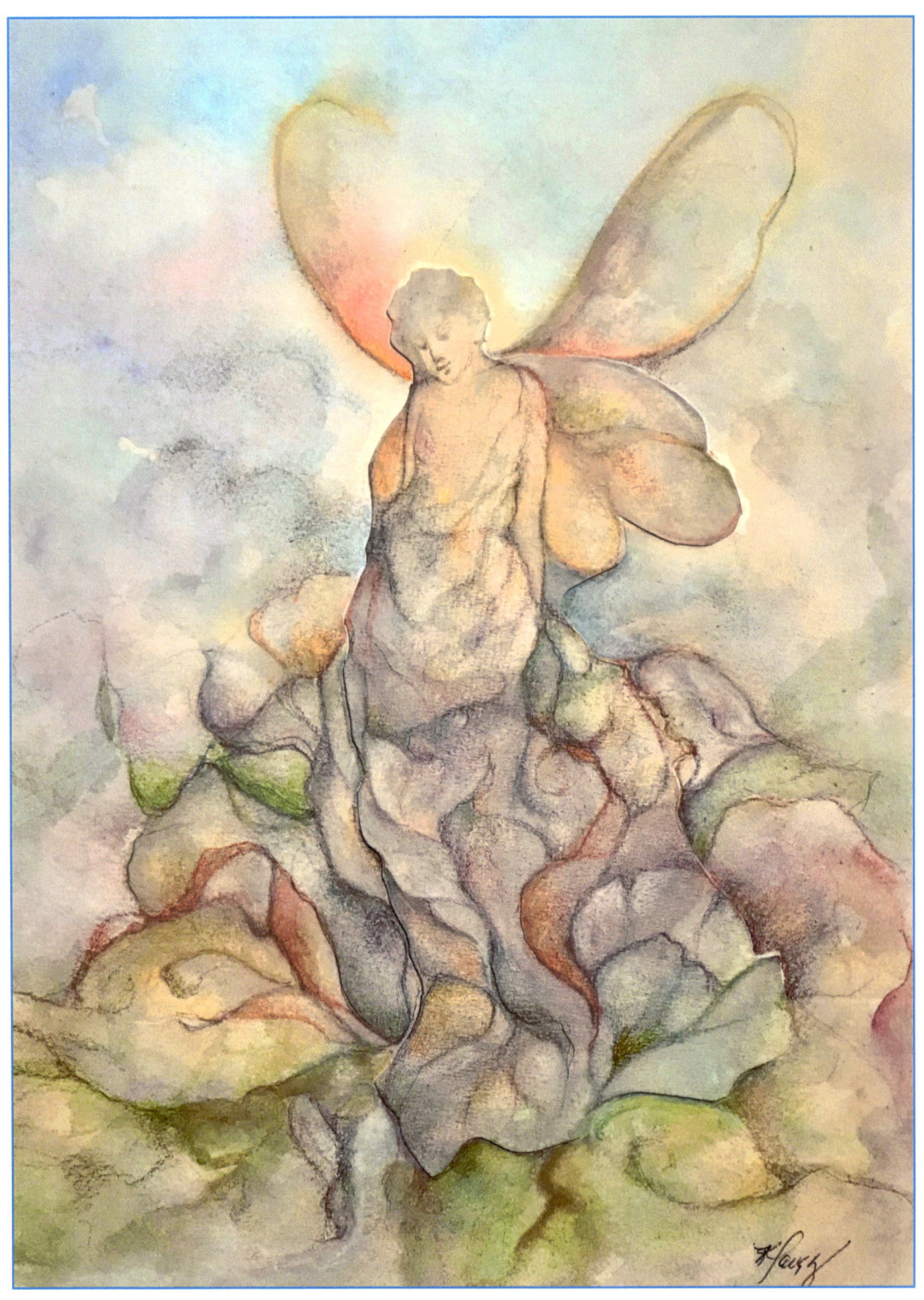

FAIRY DRESS

The flowers of the field
are the children
of sun's affection
and nature's love,

and the children of men
are the flowers of
love and compassion.

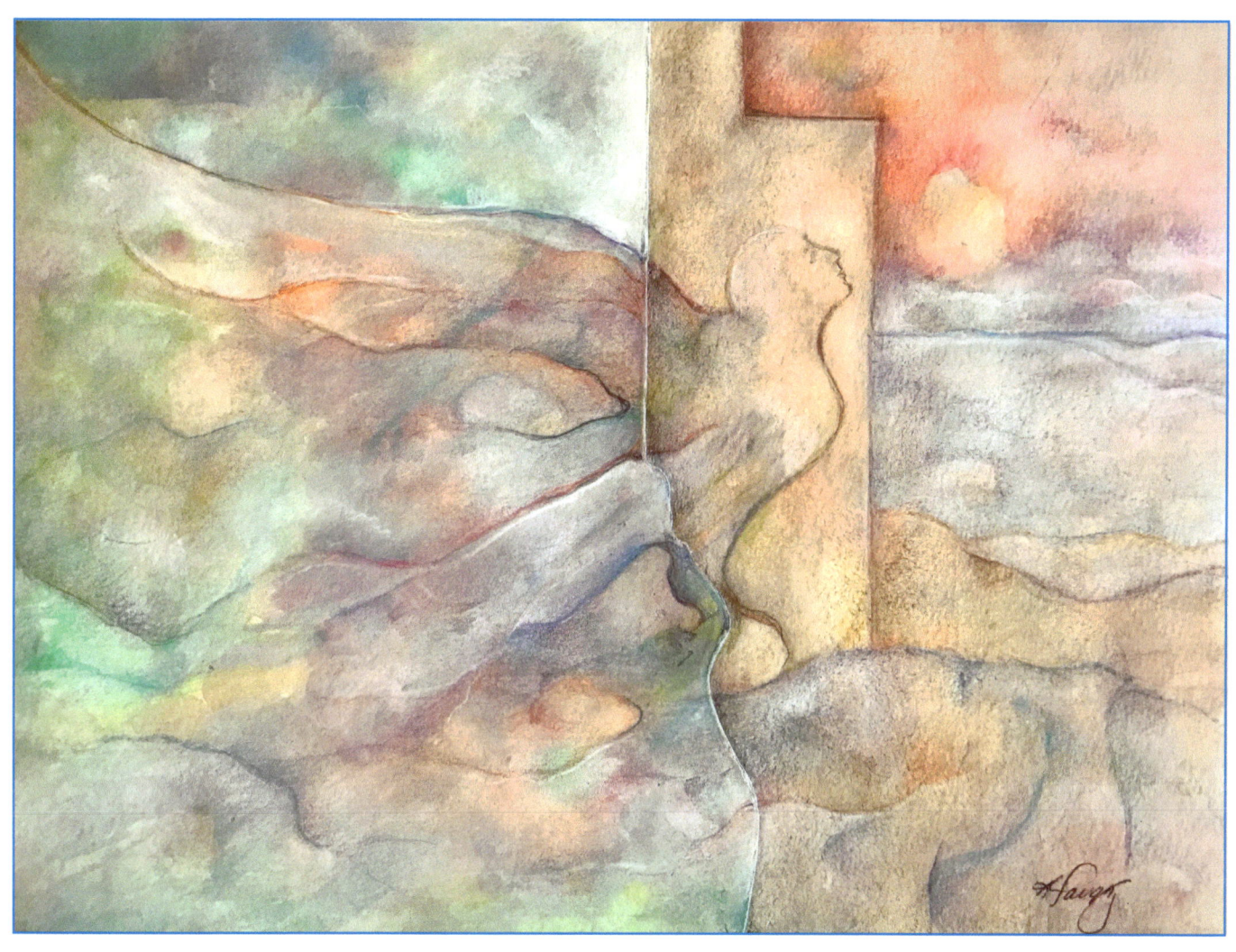

FLIGHT OF CONSCIOUSNESS

Even the most winged spirit
cannot escape physical necessity.

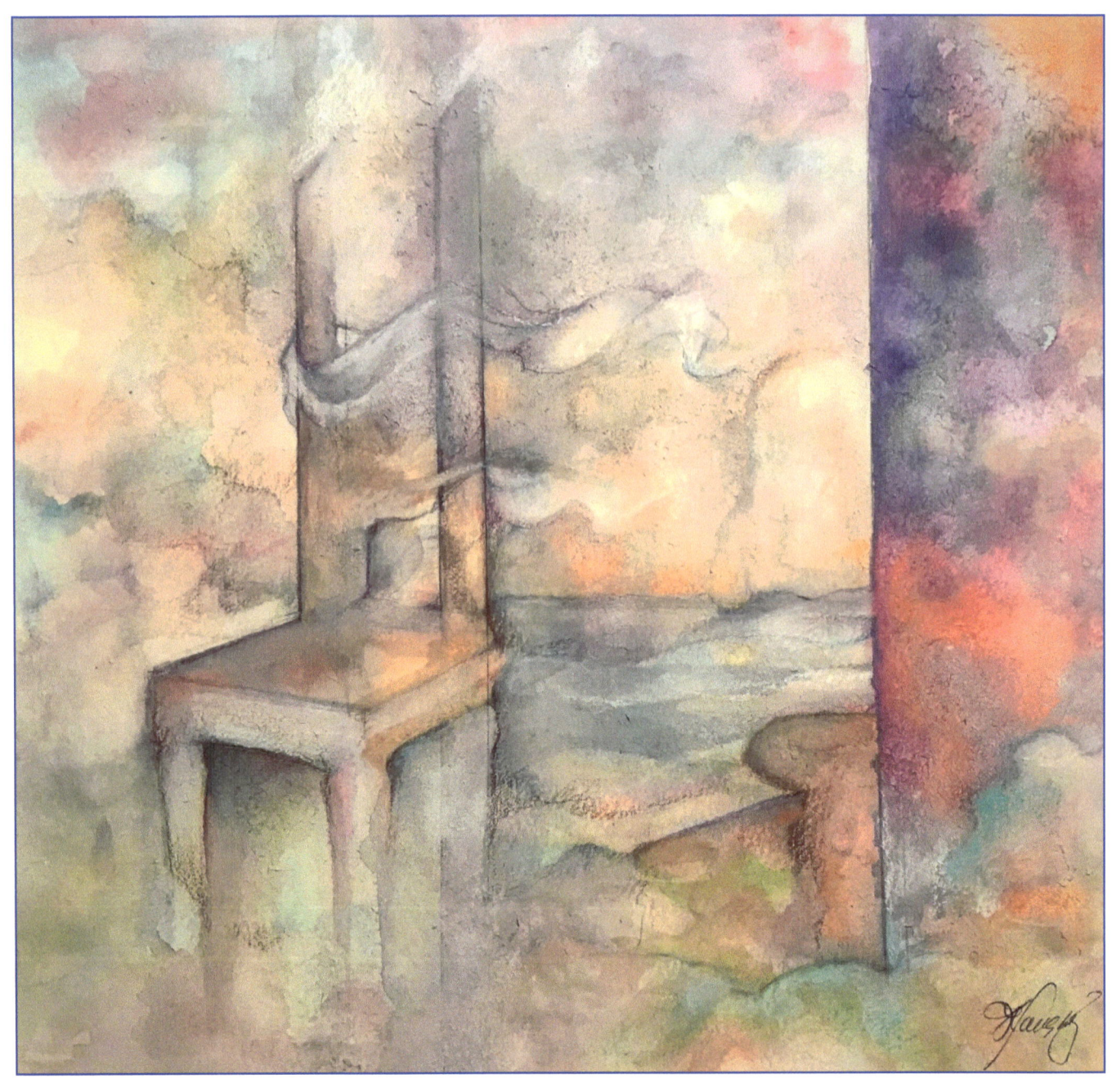

FORGOTTEN

Forgetfulness is
a form of freedom.

My loneliness was born
when men praised
my talkative faults
and blamed
my silent virtues.

10

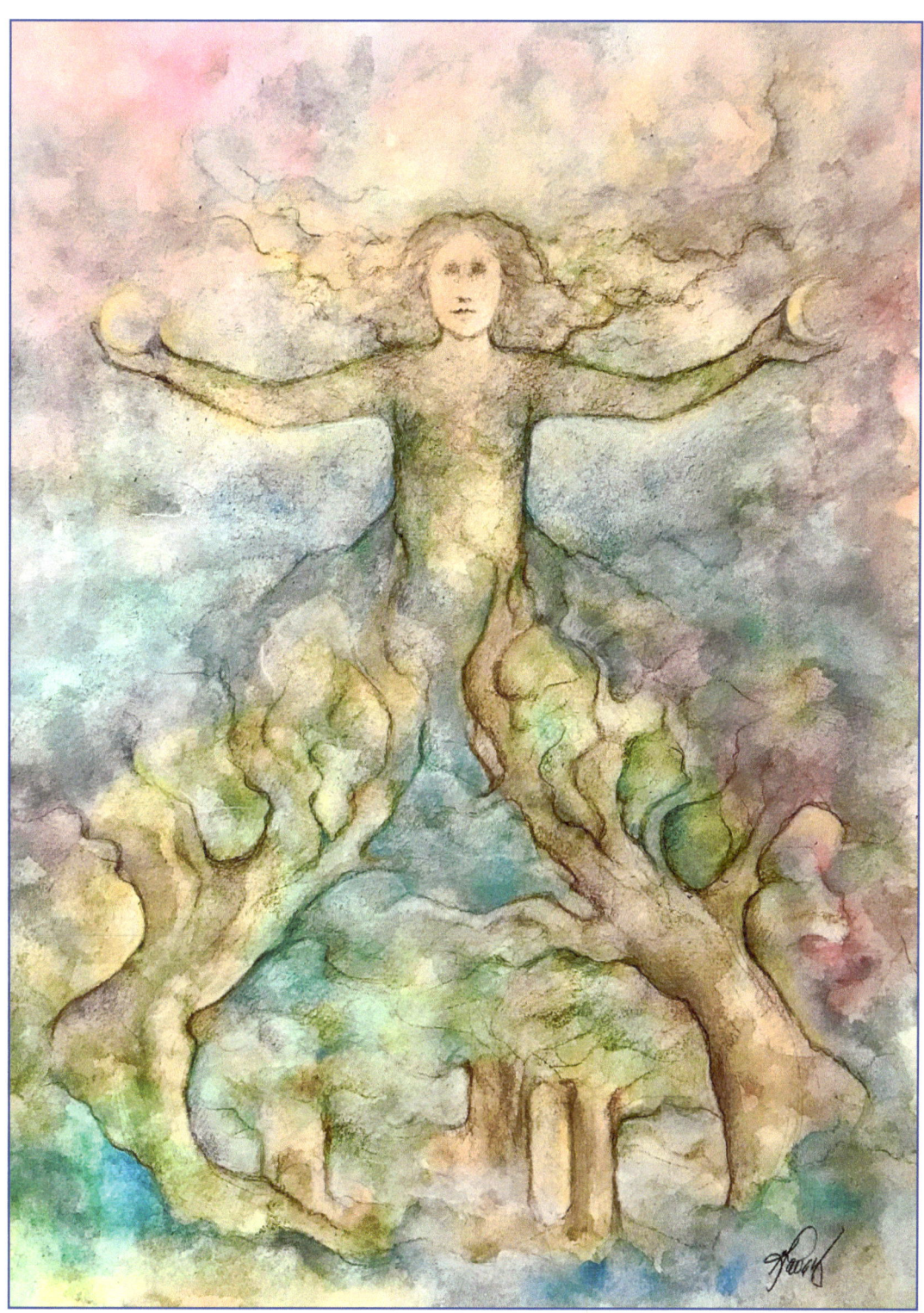

GAIA

Trees are poems
that the earth writes
upon the sky.

We fell them down
and turn them into paper
that we may record
our emptiness.

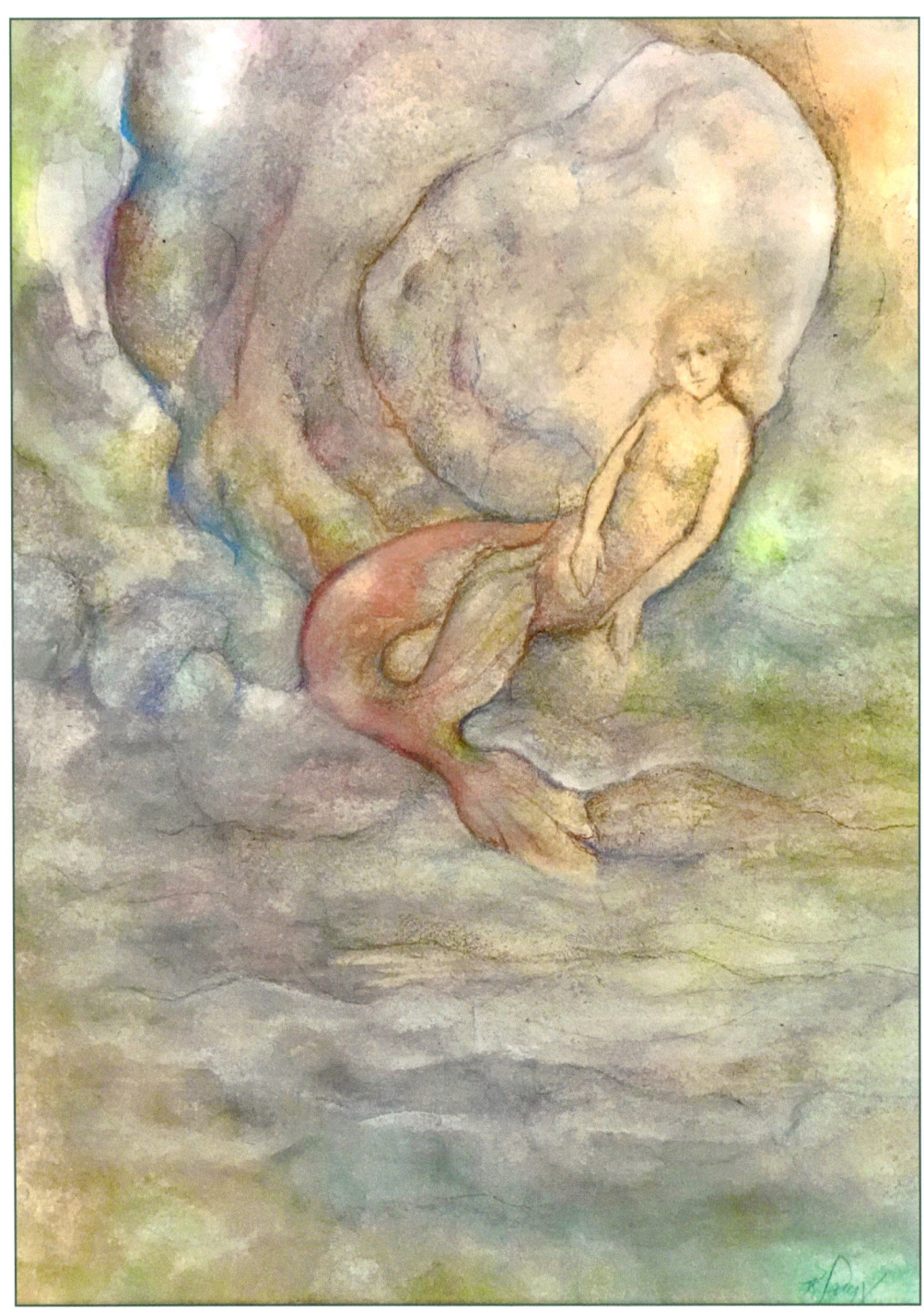

GROTTO

Thoughts have a higher dwelling place
than the visible world,
and its skies are not clouded.
There, man can glimpse
after the soul's liberation
from the world of substance.

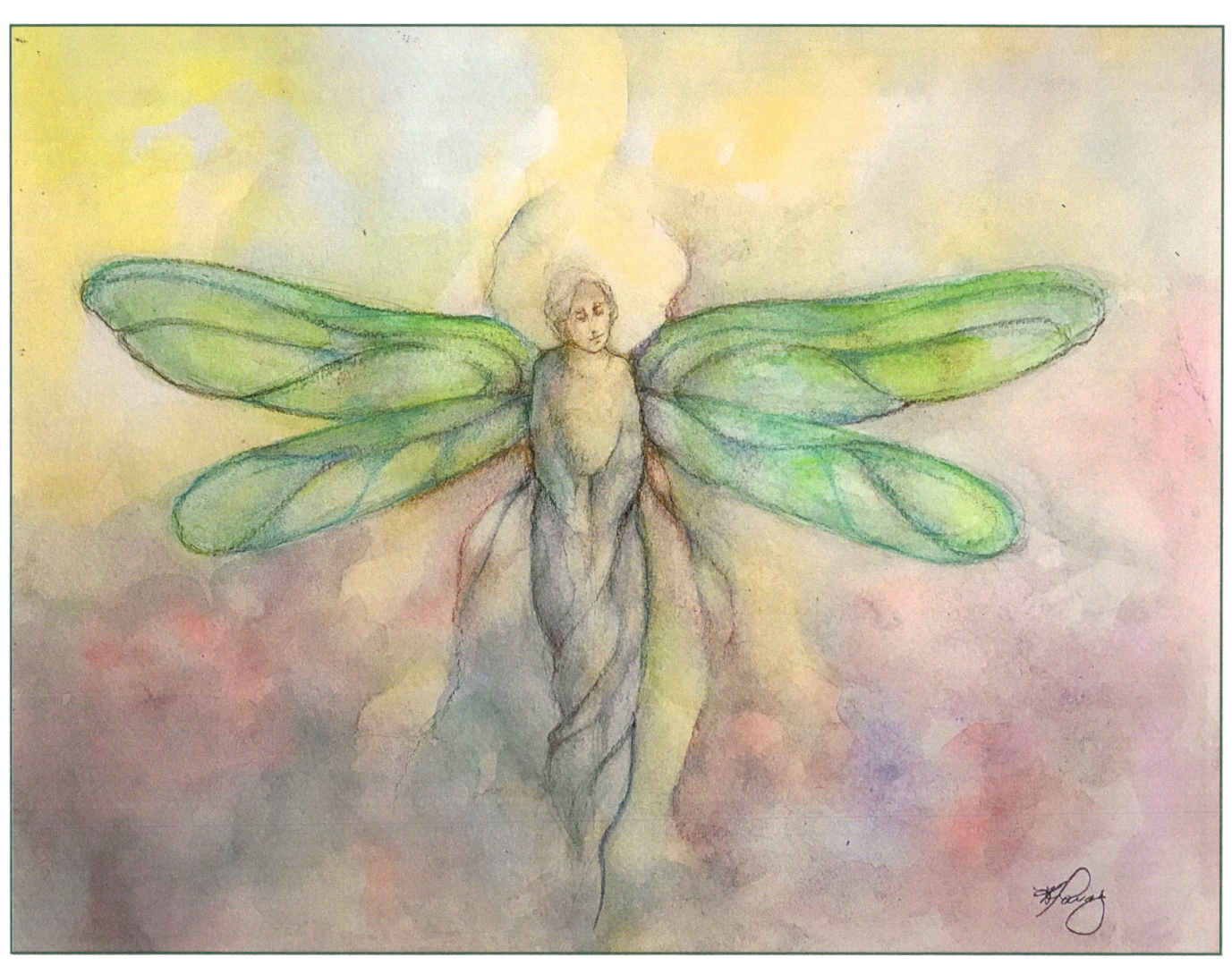

GRANDMOTHER DRAGONFLY

Everything in nature
bespeaks the mother.
The sun is the mother of earth
and gives its nourishment of heat;
it never leaves the universe at night
until it has put the earth to sleep,
to the song of the sea,
the hymn of the birds and brooks.

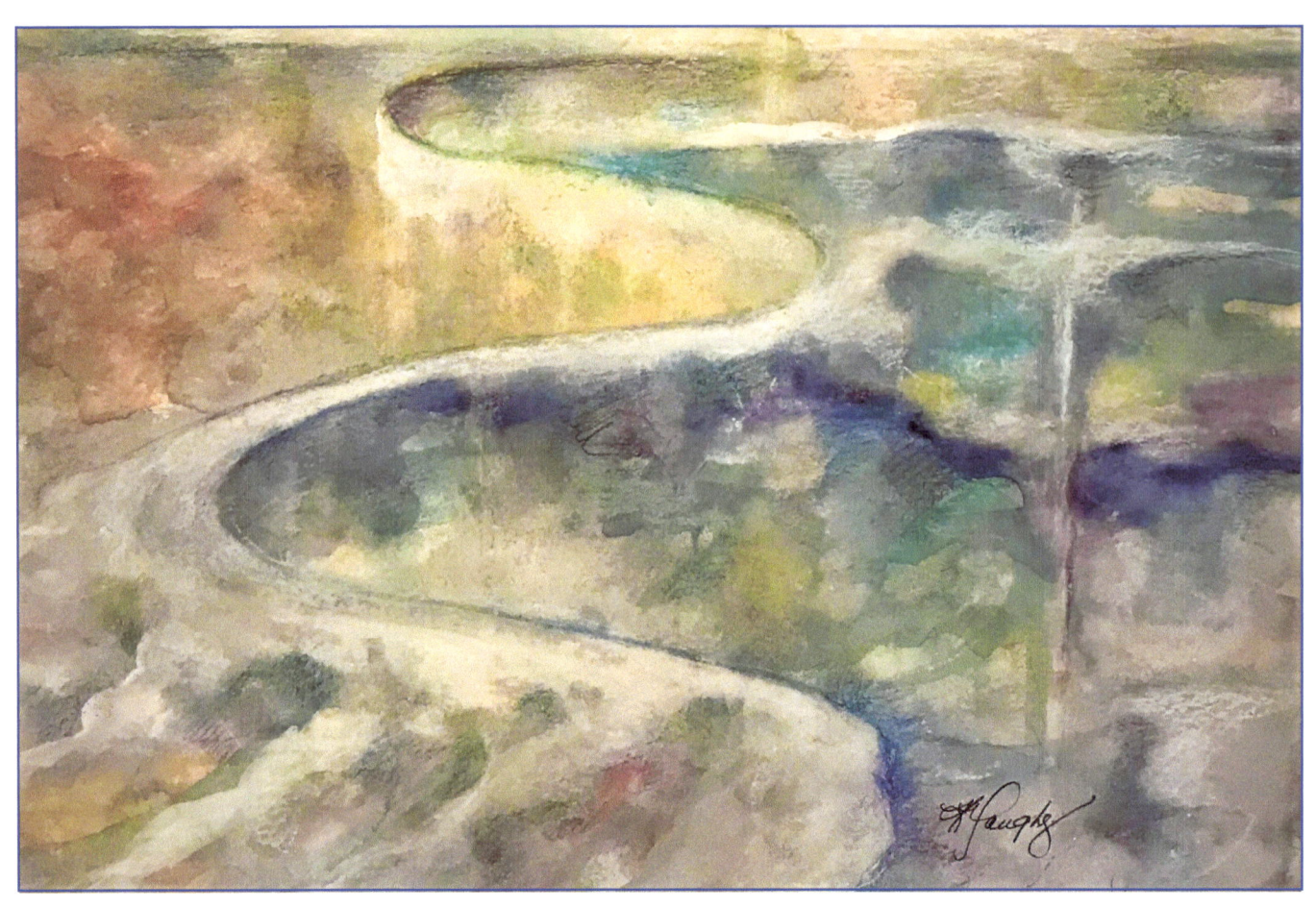

HIDDEN COVE

During the ebb
I wrote a line upon the sand,
committing to it all
that is in my soul and mind;
I returned at the ebb
to read and ponder upon it;
I found naught upon it
but my ignorance.

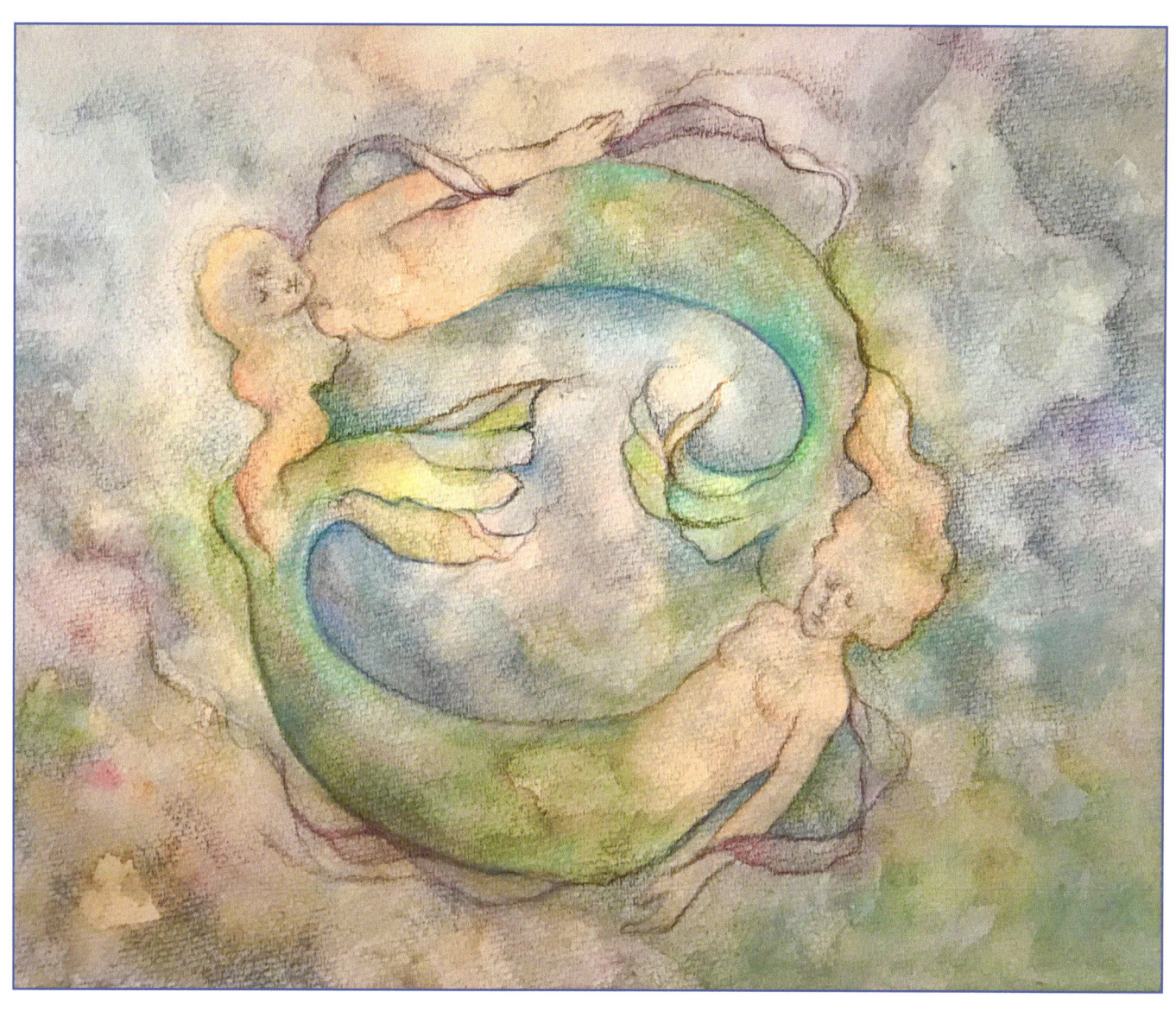

PISCES

The hidden well spring of your soul
must needs rise and run
murmuring to the sea;
and the treasure
of your infinite depths
should be revealed to your eyes.
And seek not the depths
of your knowledge
with staff or sounding line.
For the self is a sea
boundless and measureless.

15

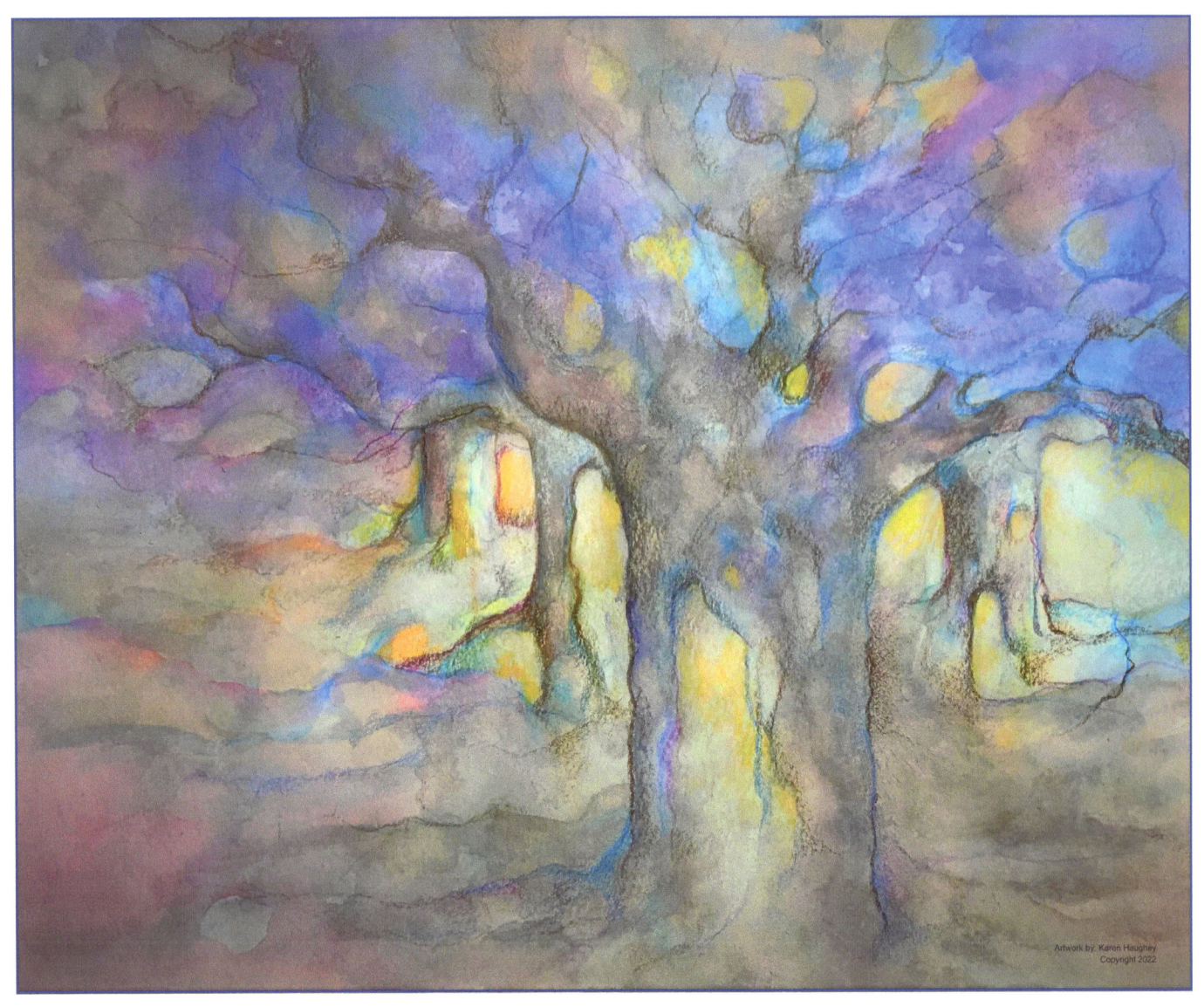

LAVENDER WOODS

Where shall you seek beauty,
and how shall you find her
unless she herself be
your way and your guide?

LOVE BIRDS

Friendship is always a sweet responsibility,
never an opportunity.

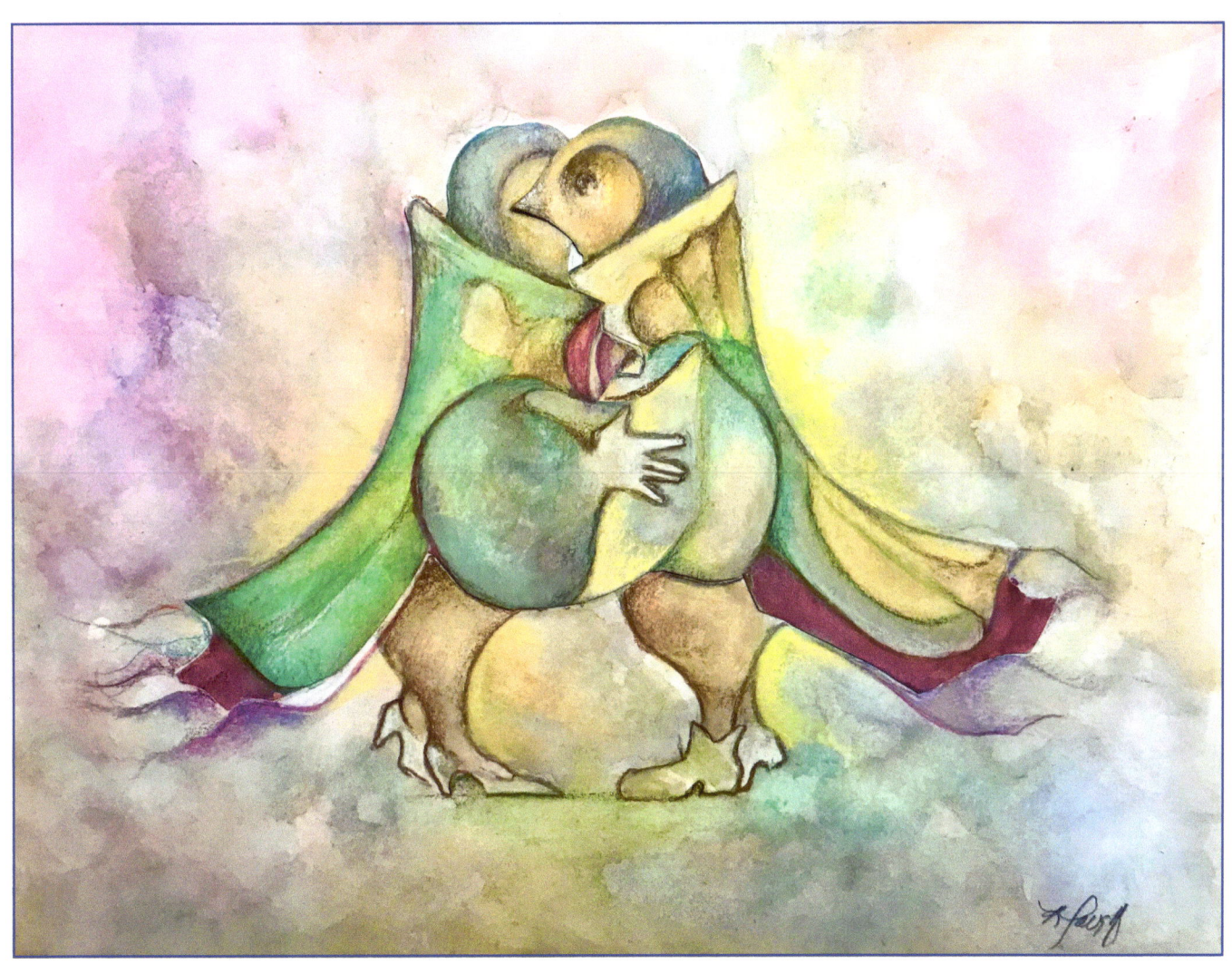

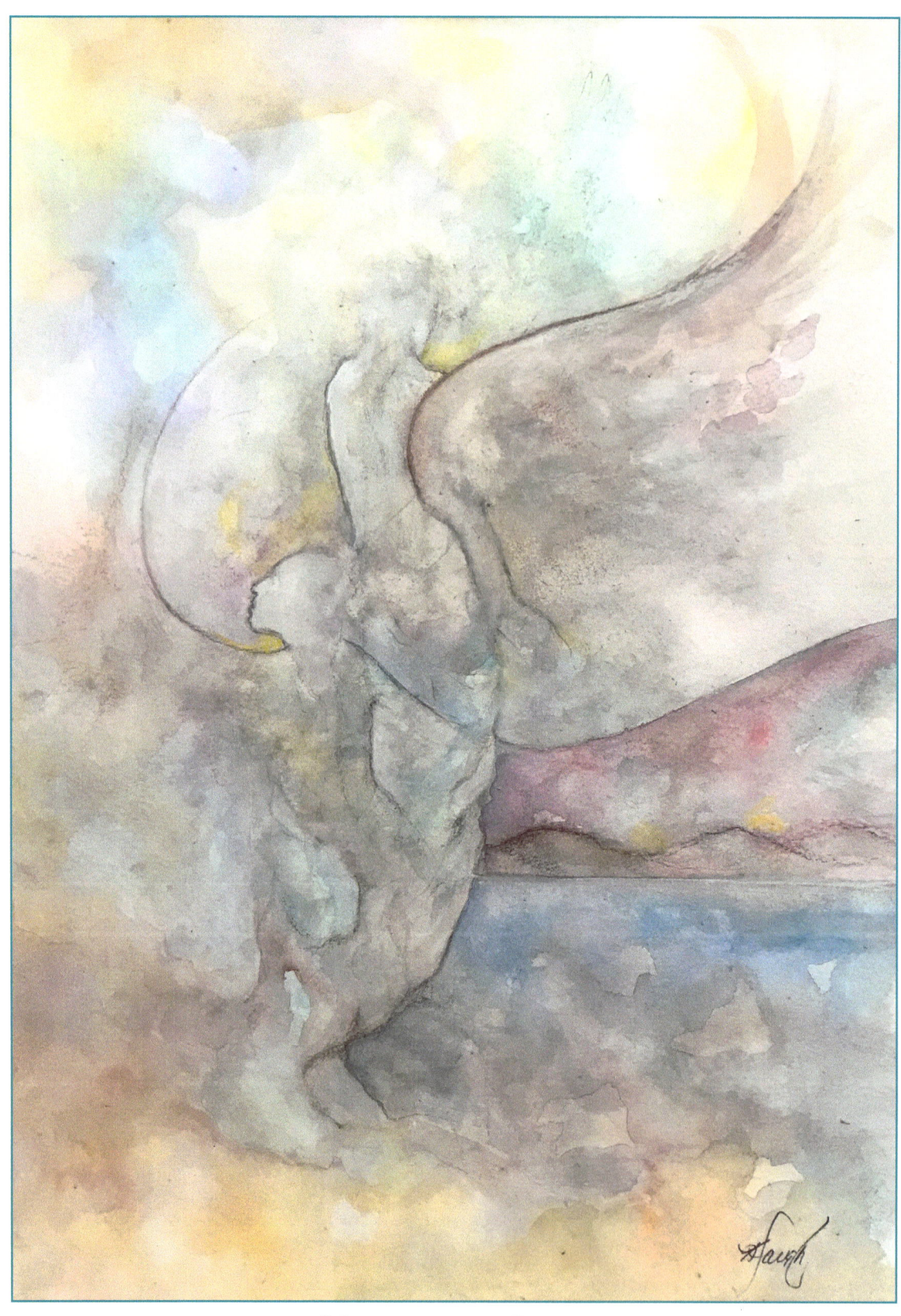

MANKIND AND SPIRIT

The reason why the soul exists is folded in the soul itself.
No painting could show its essence, nor manifest its true self.

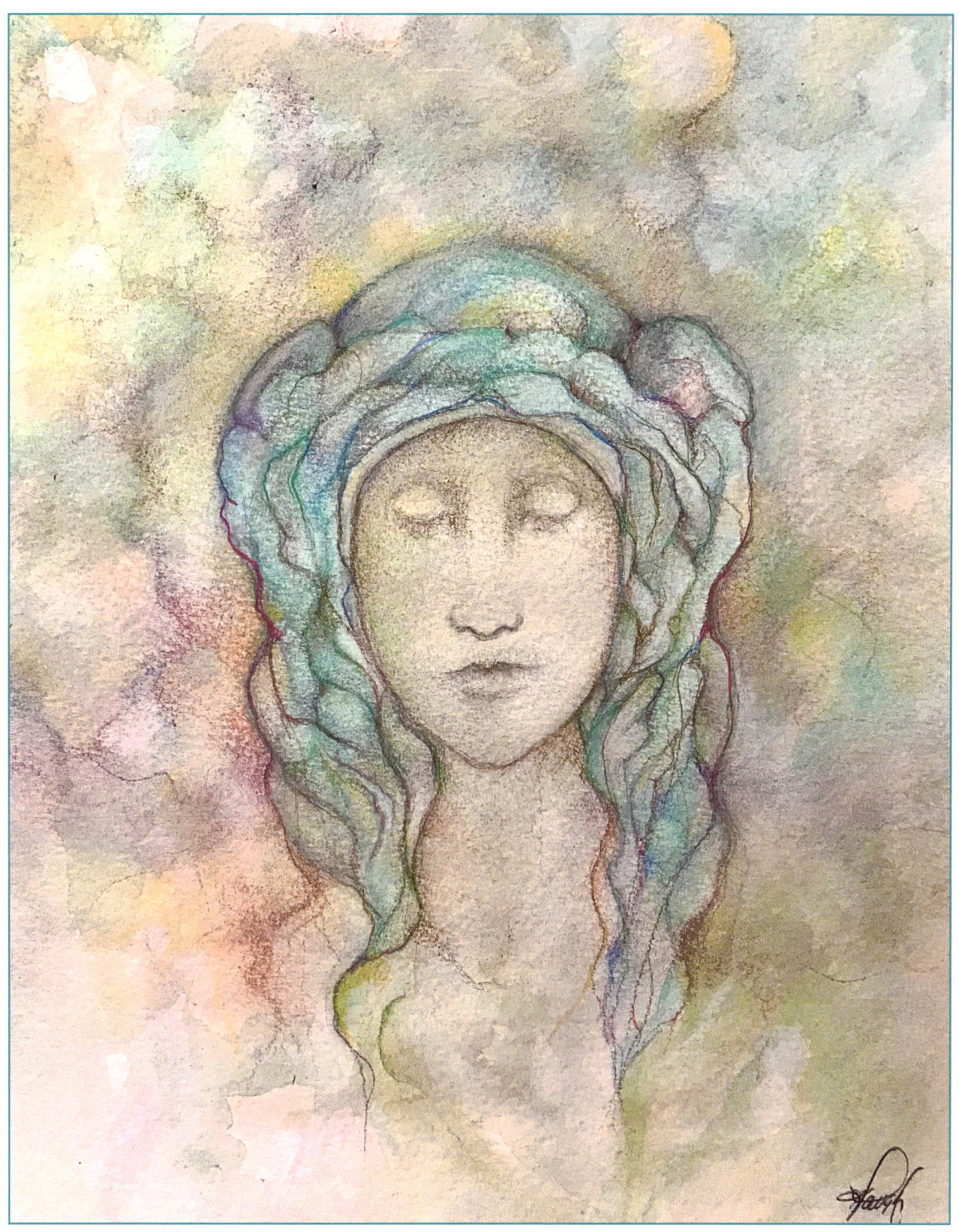

MERMAID

Perhaps the sea's definition of a shell is the pearl.
Perhaps time's definition of coal is the diamond.

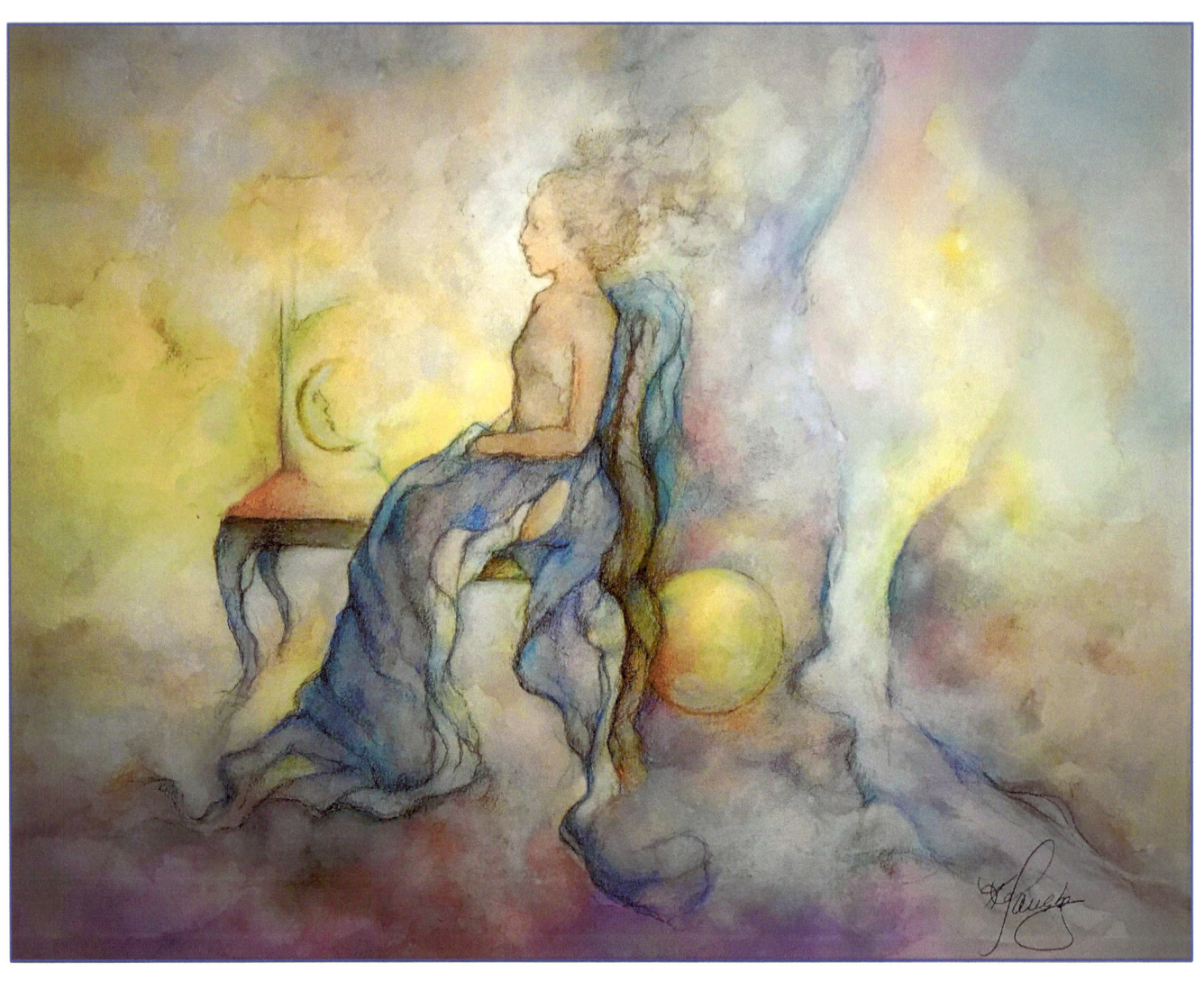

NIGHT CONVERSING WITH THE MOON

There is a space between imagination and attainment
that may only be traversed by ones longing.

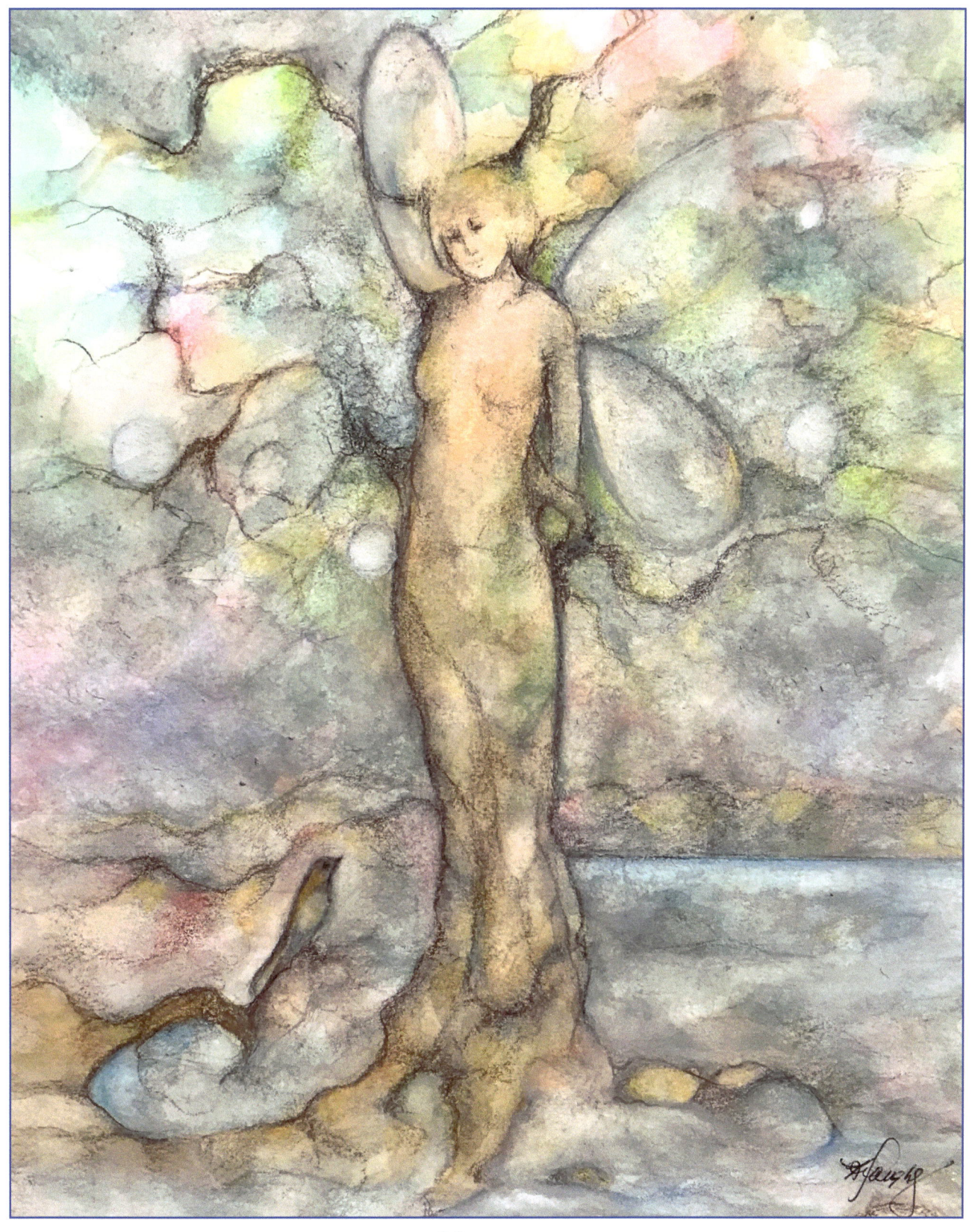

NESTING

Should a tree write its autobiography,
it would not be unlike the history of humanity.

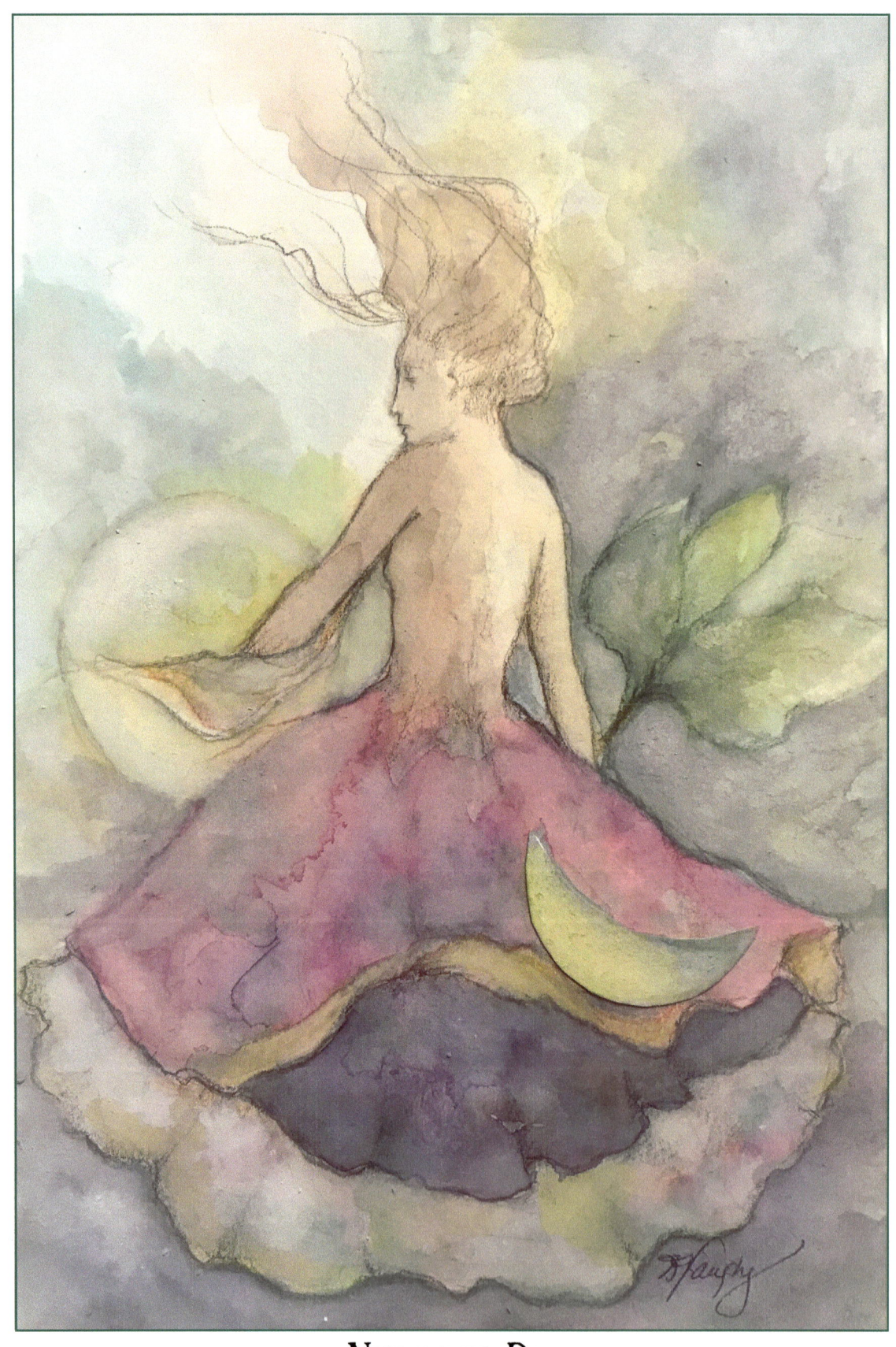

NIGHT INTO DAY

One may not reach the dawn save by the path of the night.

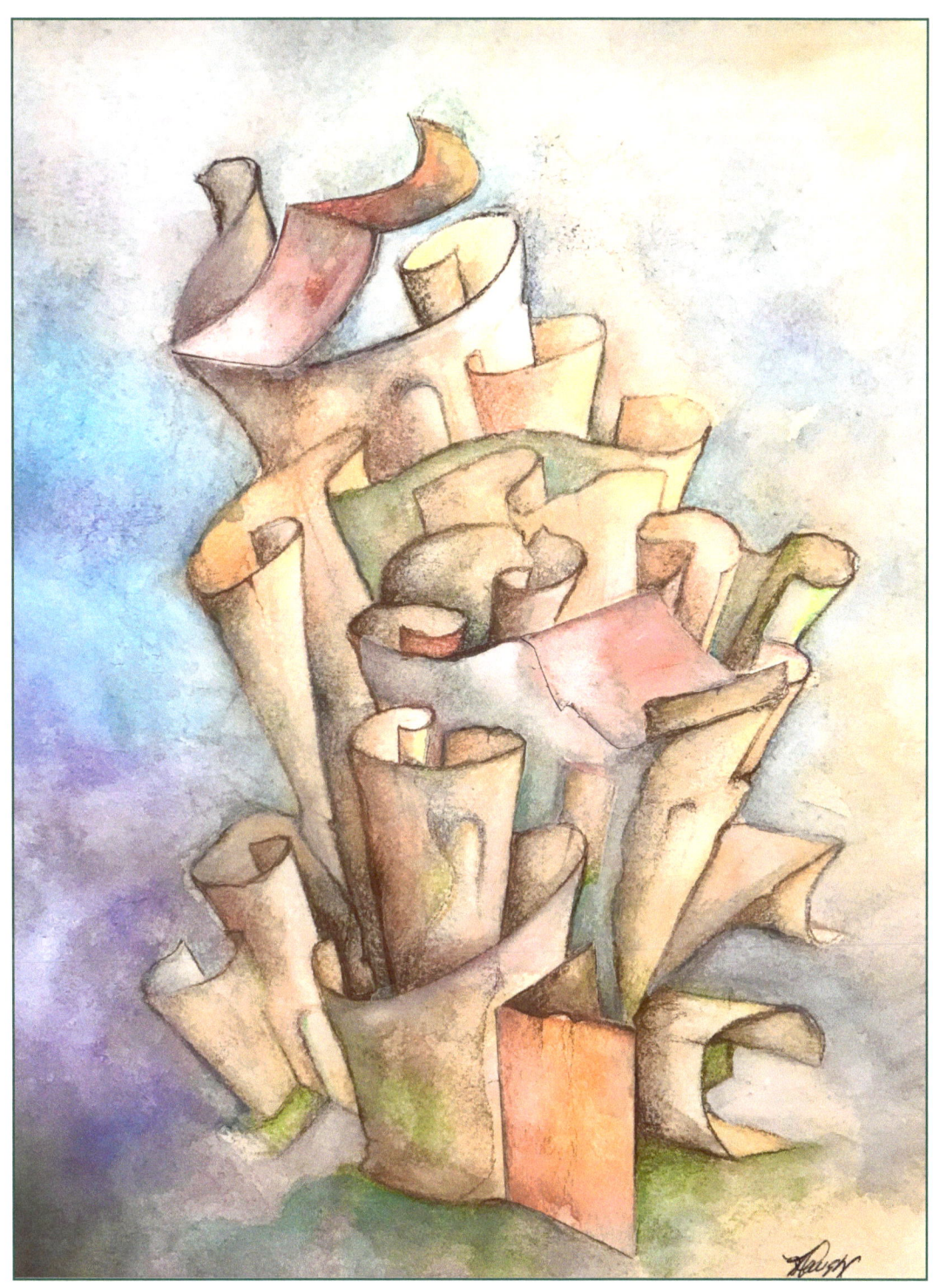

Paper Houses

For even as you have
home-comings in your twilight,
so has the wanderer in you,
the ever distant and alone.
Your house is your larger body.

It grows in the sun,
and sleeps in the
stillness of the night;
and it is not dreamless.

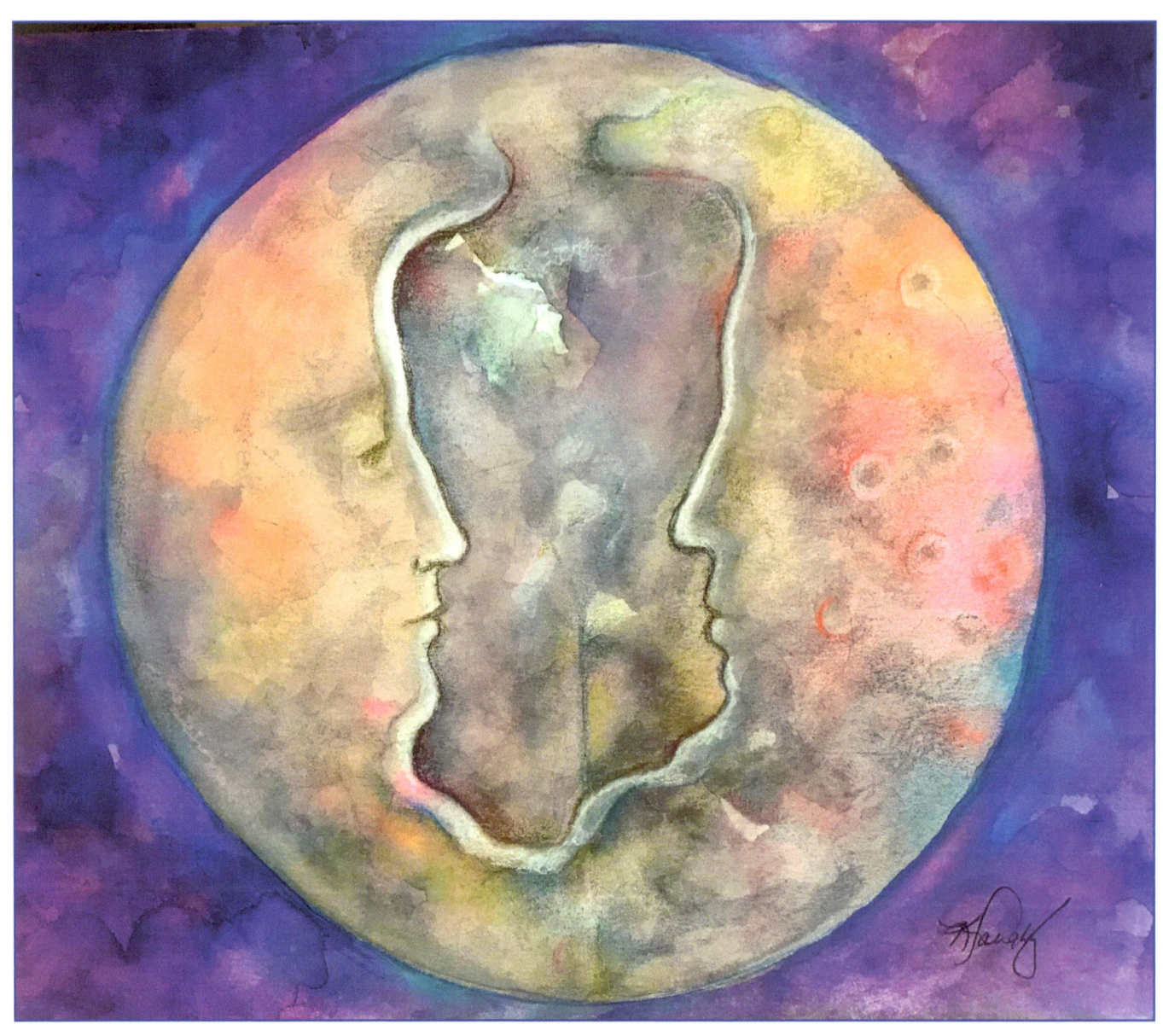

PERCEPTION

How unjust to themselves are those
who turn their backs to the sun,
and do not see the shadows
of their physical selves upon the earth.

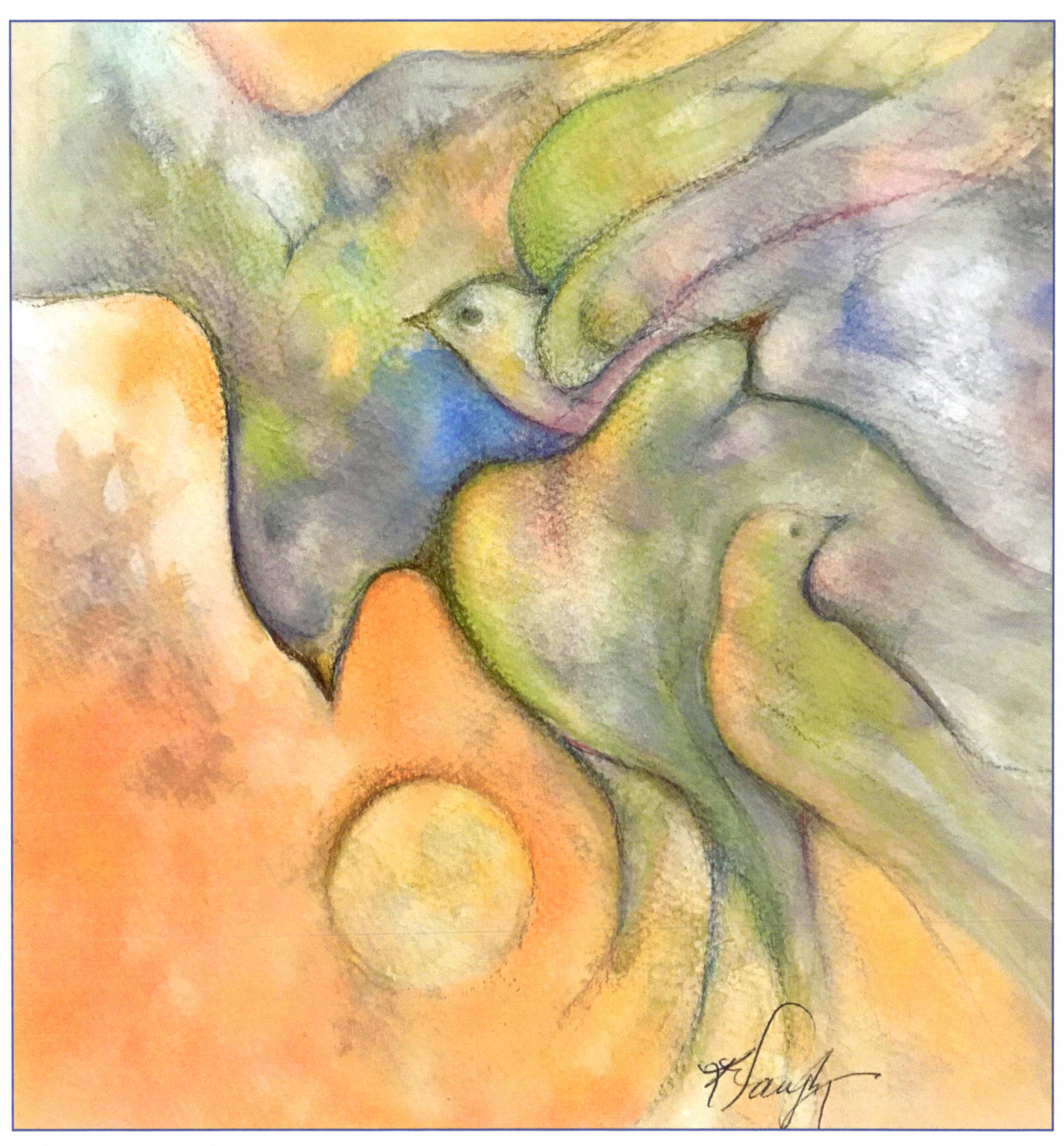

PRAYER BIRDS

I cannot teach you
how to pray in words,
and I cannot teach you
the prayer of the seas,
forests, or the mountains.
But who are born of the
mountains, forests and seas
can their prayer be in your heart.

25

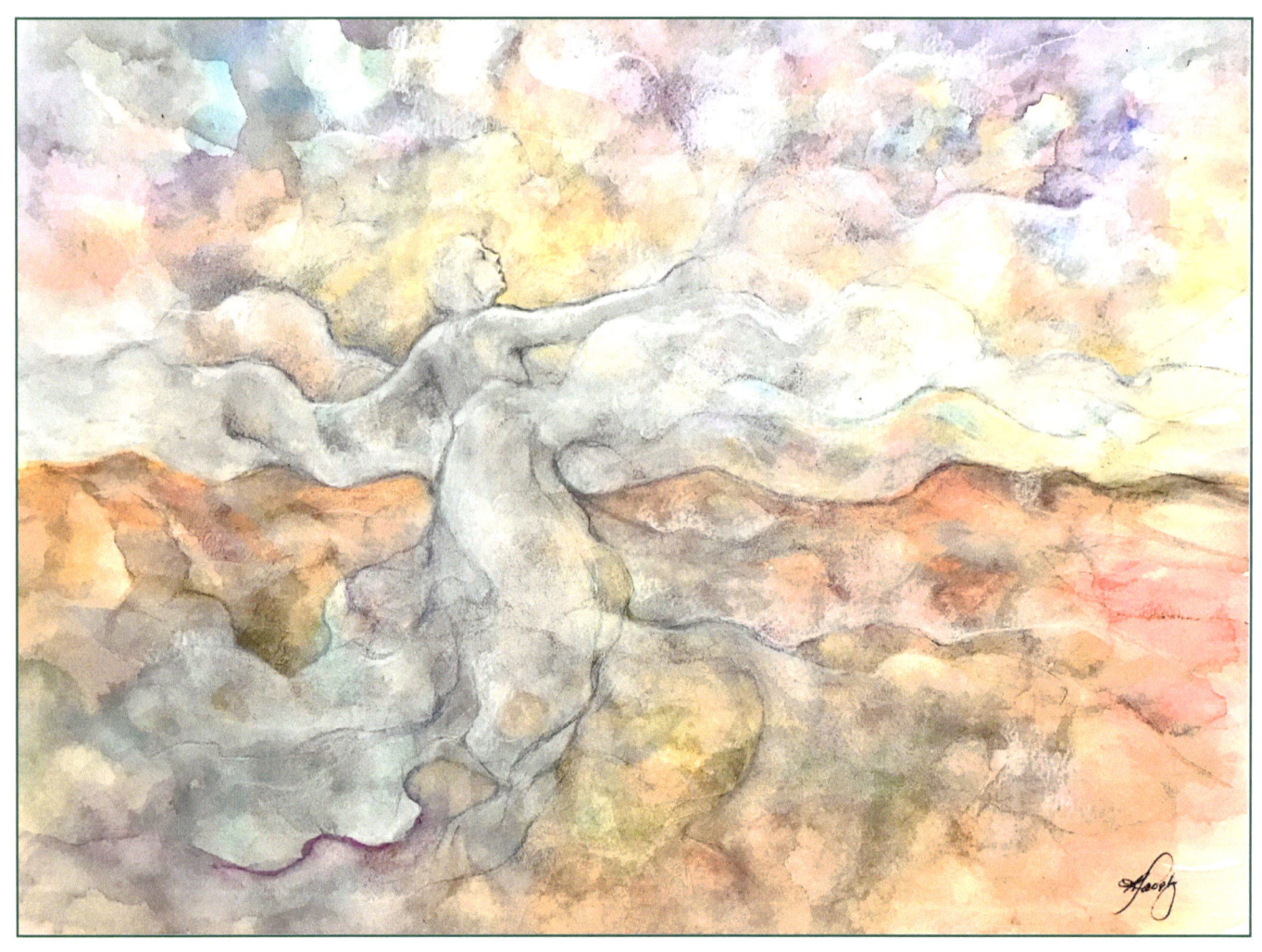

WIND CHASE

If you reveal your secrets to the wind,
you should not blame the wind
for revealing them to the trees.

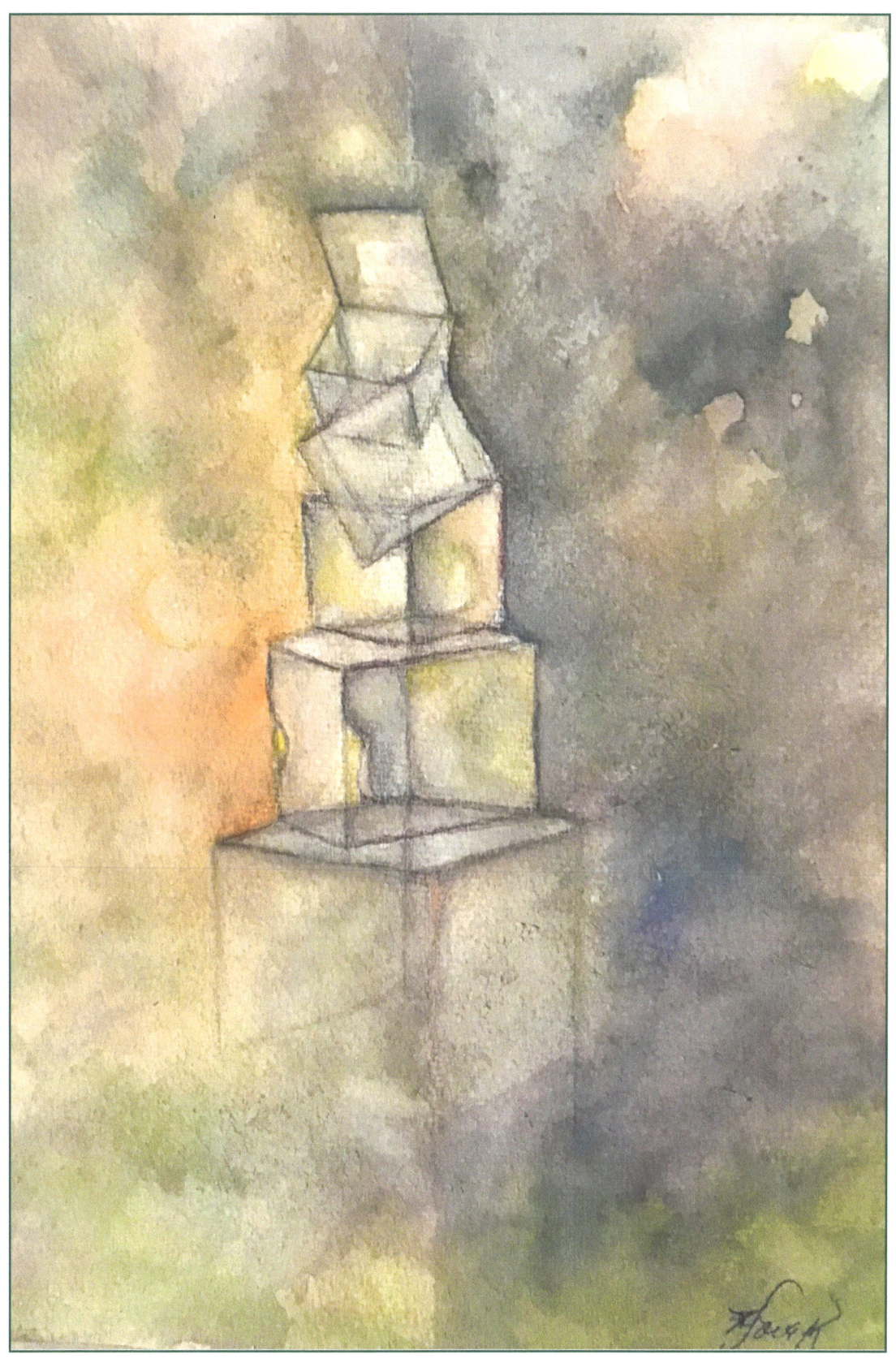

WISHING BOXES

We choose our joys and our sorrows long before we experience them.

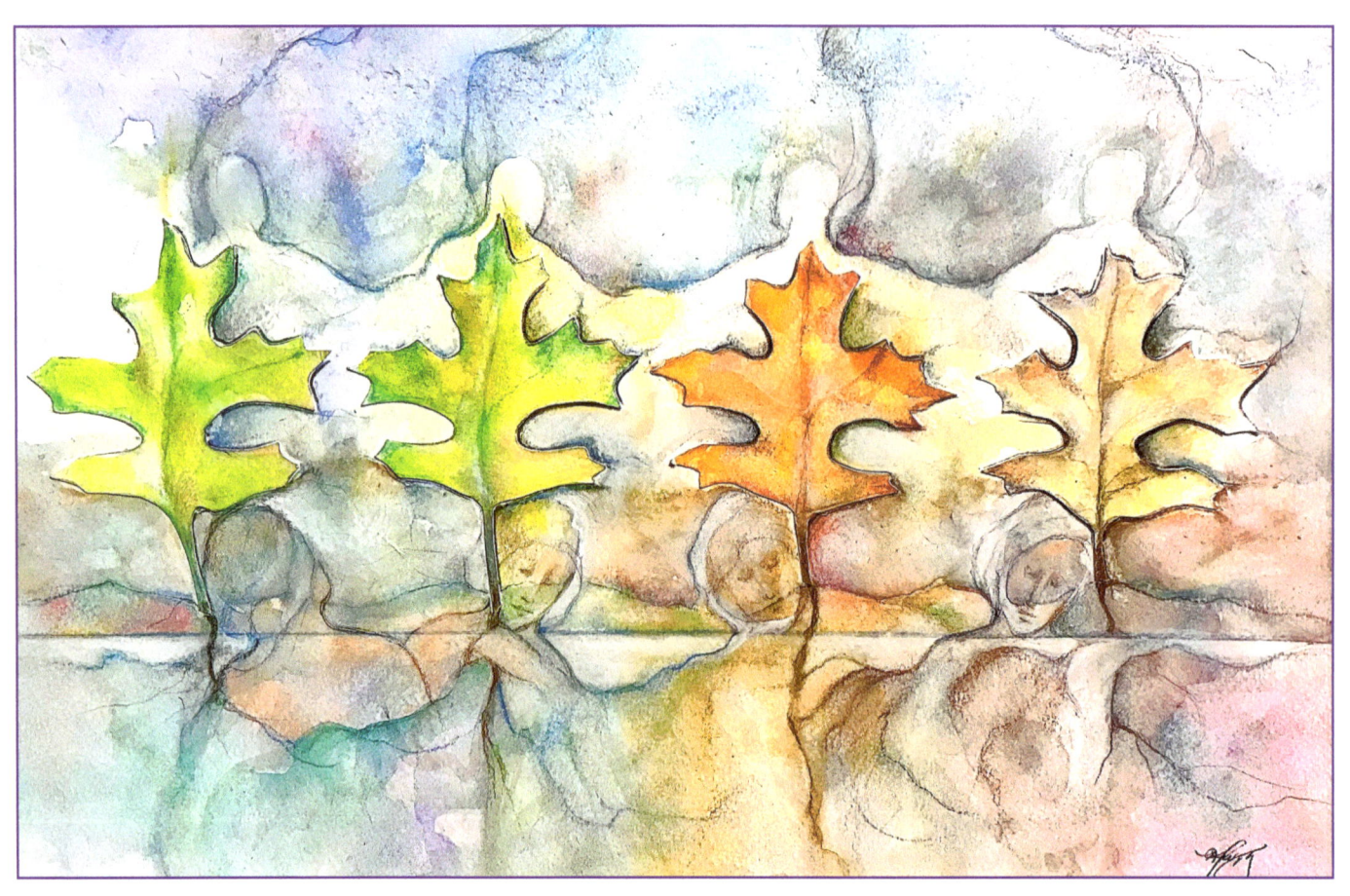

Transitions

But within your thought
you must measure
time into seasons,
let each season encircle
all of the other seasons.
And let today embrace
the past with remembrance,
and the future with longing.

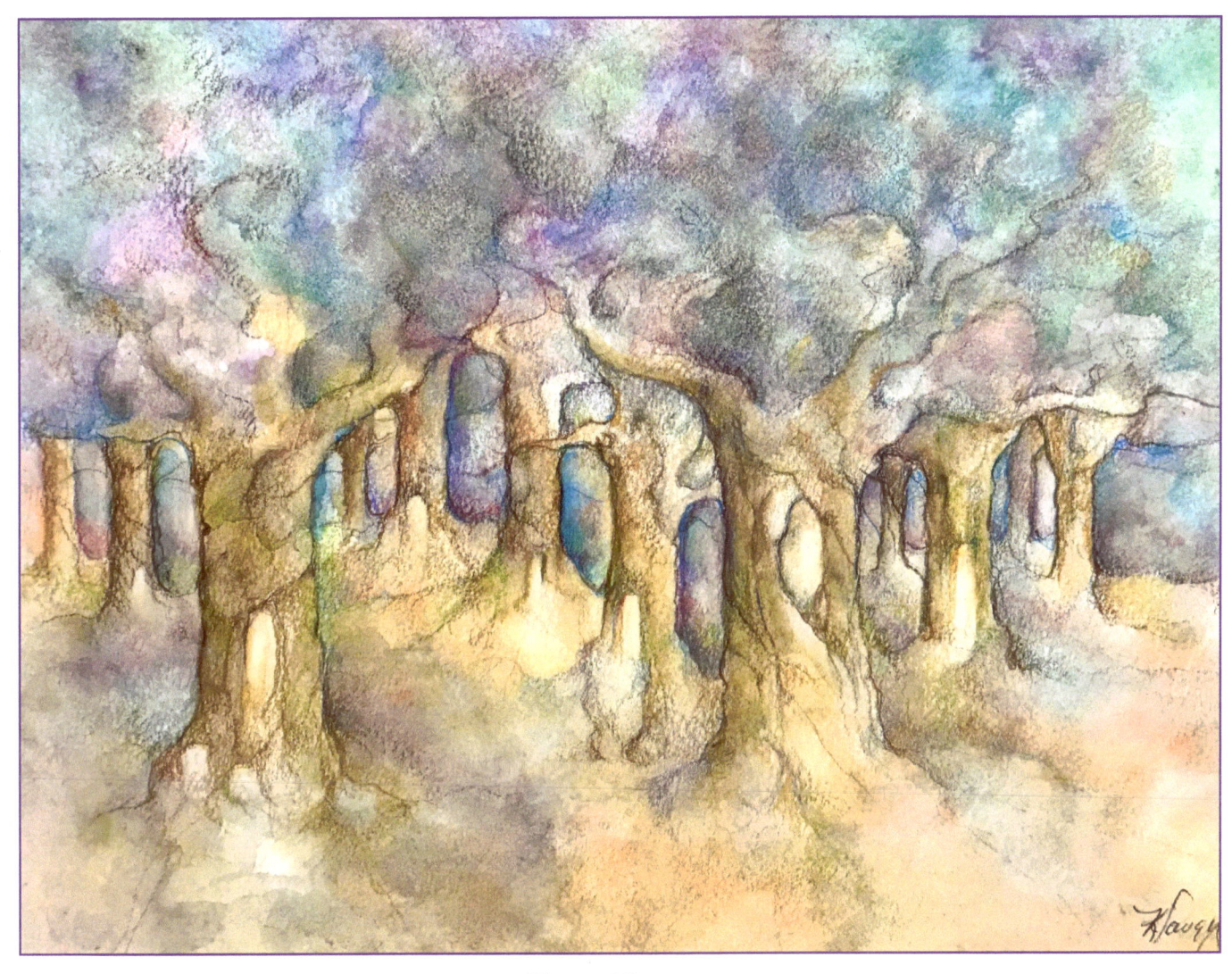

TREE HOUSES

If winter should
say that spring
is in my heart,
who would
believe winter?

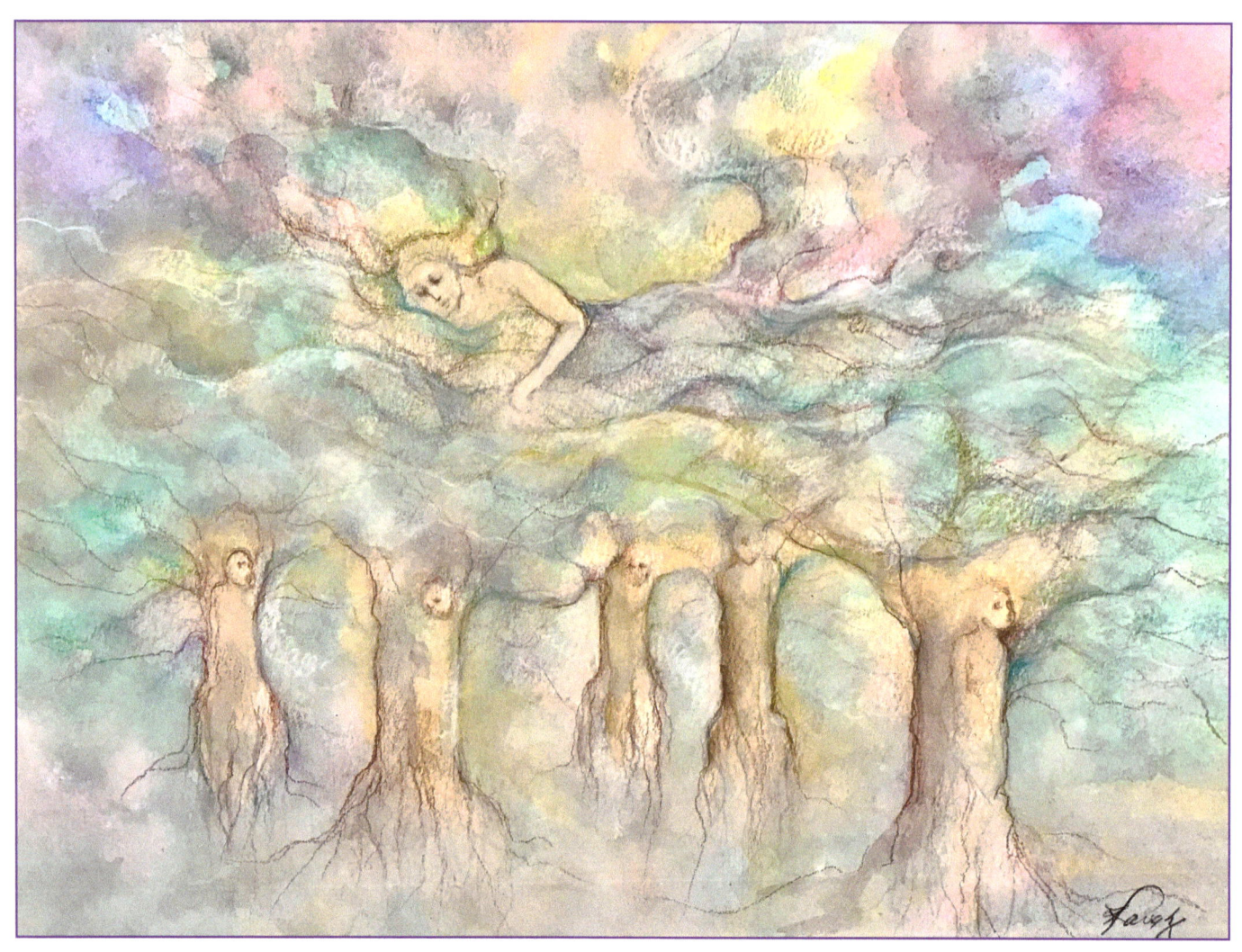

TREE SECRETS

Every seed is a longing.

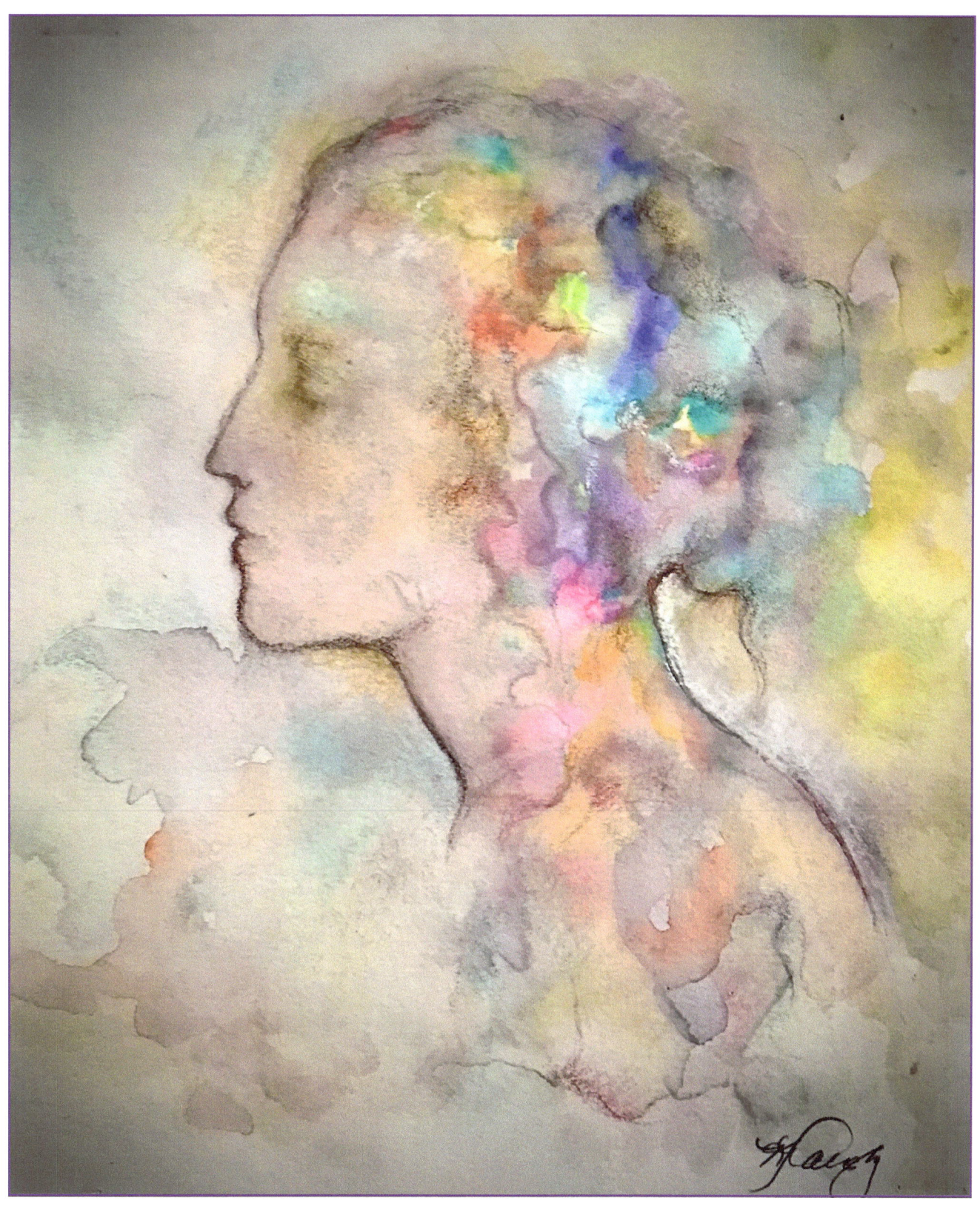

MEMORIES

A women may veil
her face with a smile.

31

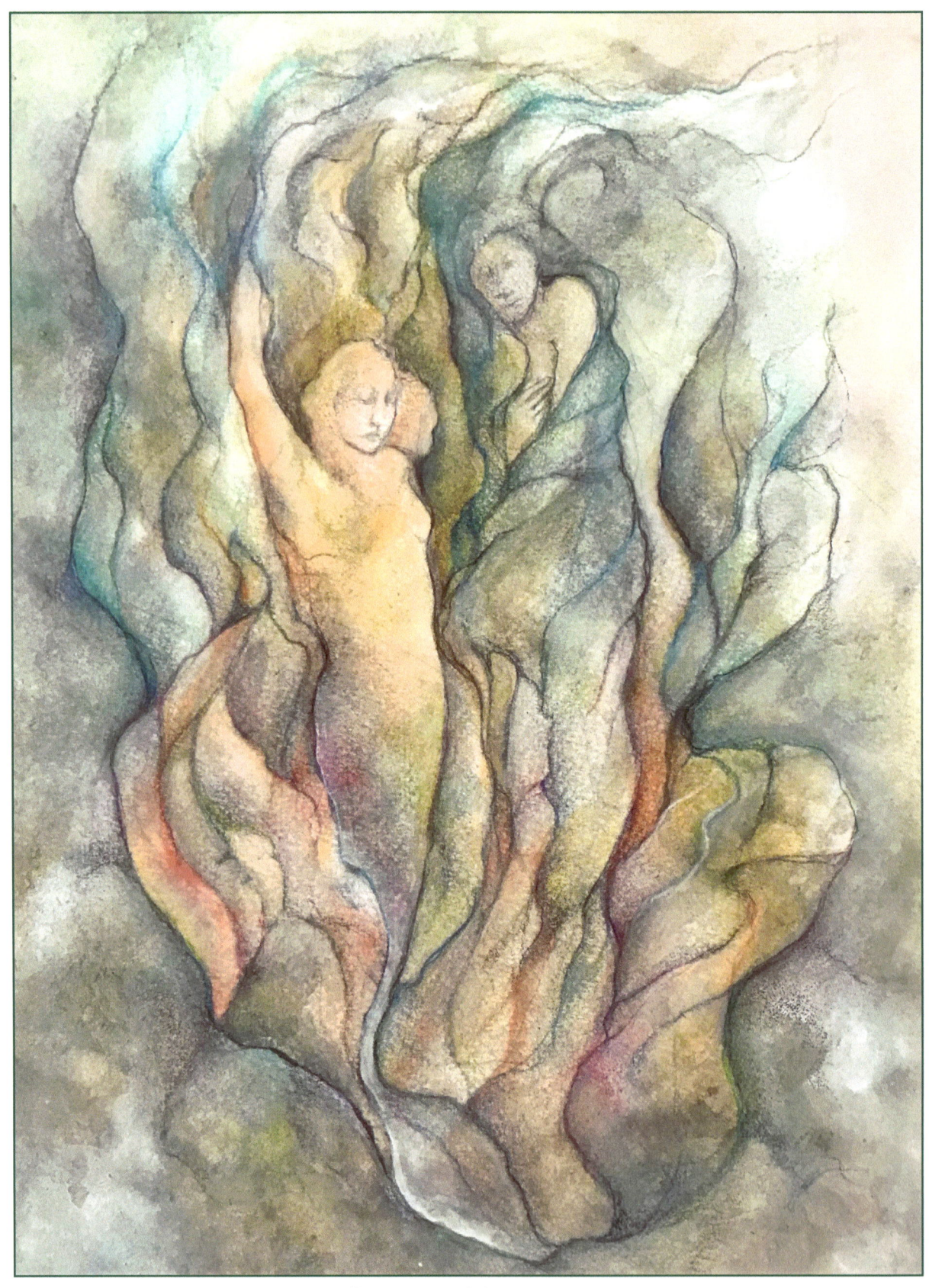

SLEEPING MERMAIDS

The real in us is silent; the acquired is talkative.

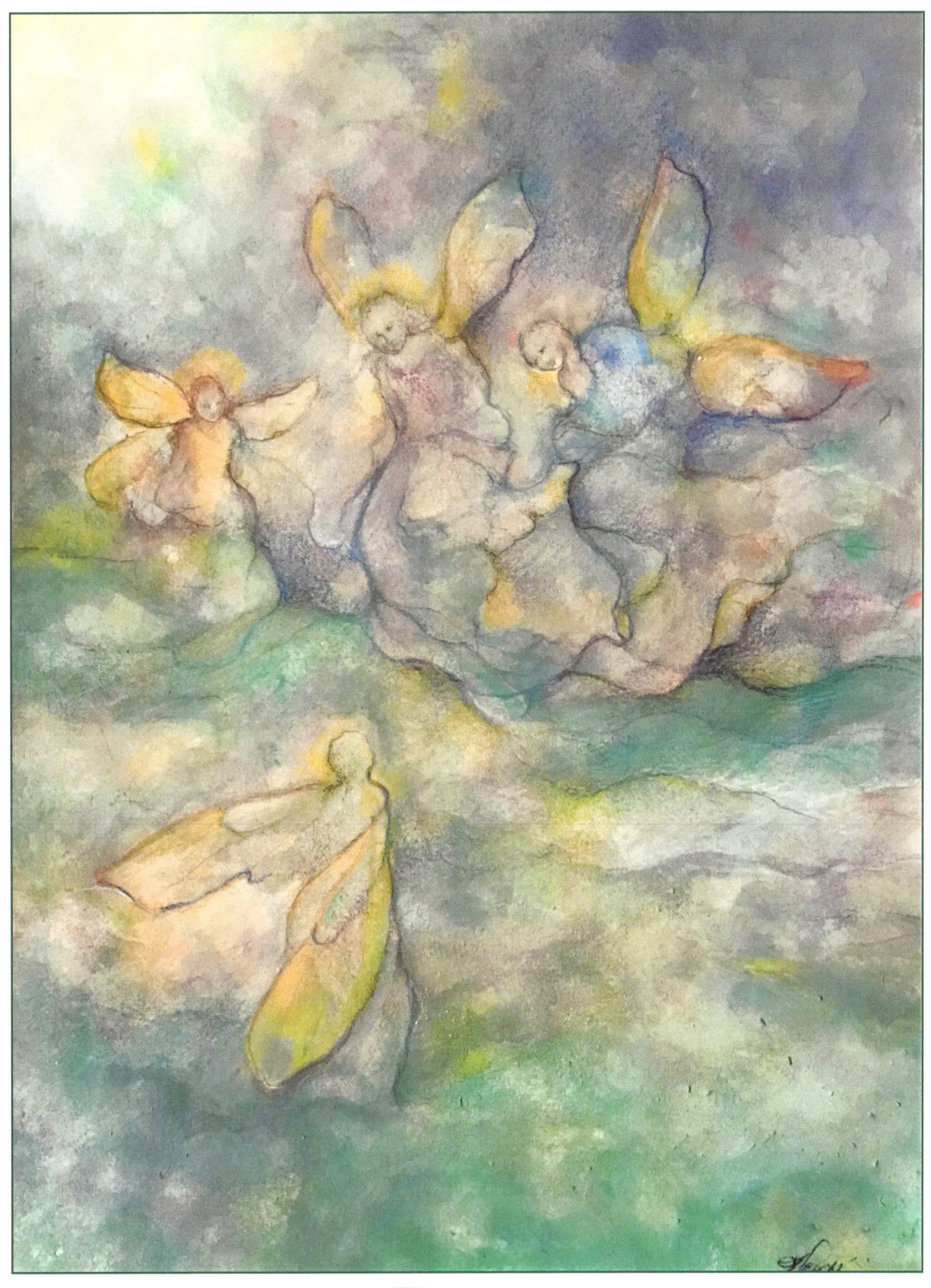

WELCOMING

Remembrance is a form of meeting.

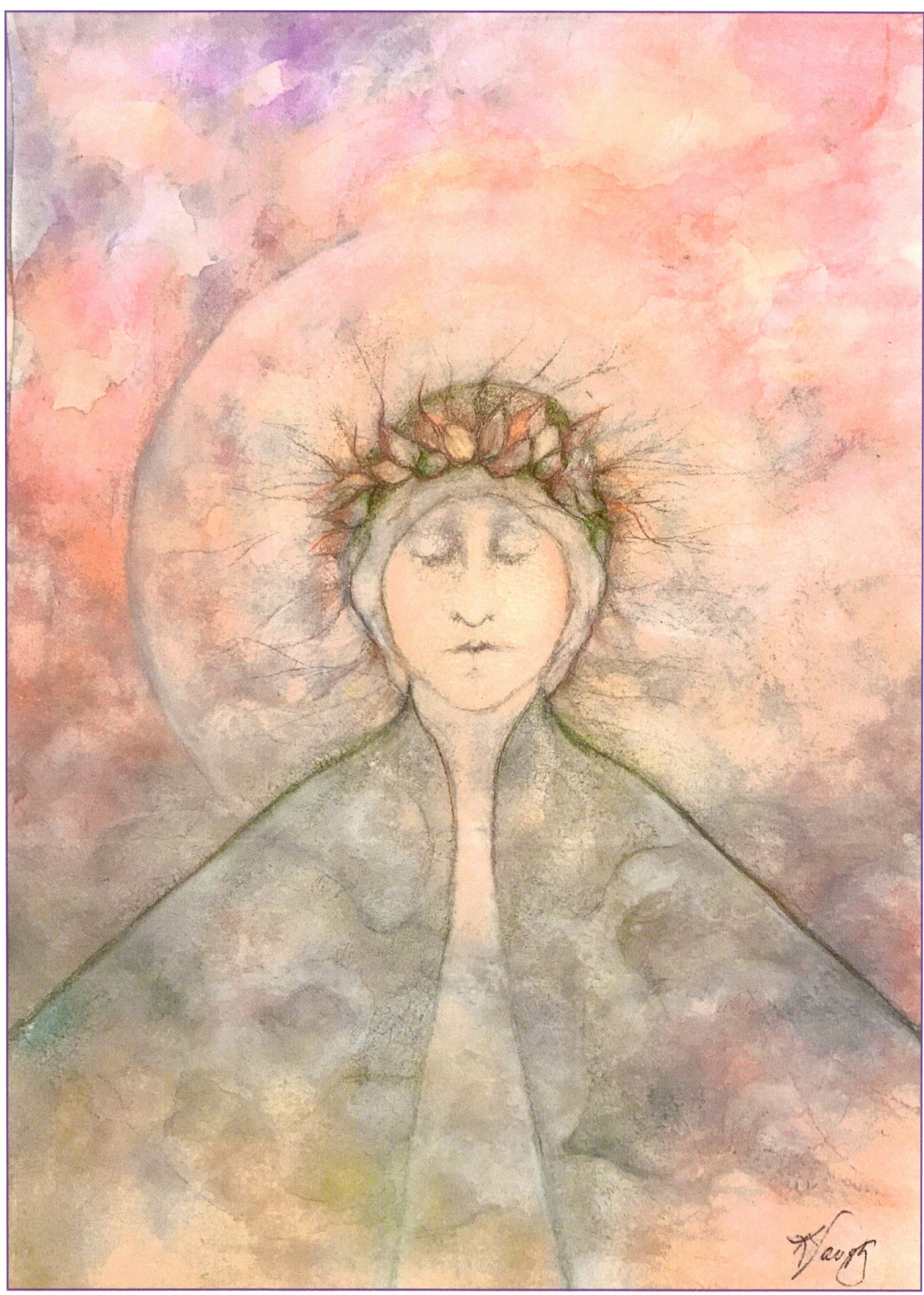

AUTUMN SPIRIT

In the Autumn I gathered
all of my sorrows and
buried them in my garden.
And when April returned,
spring came to wed the earth
and there grew in my
garden beautiful flowers
unlike all other flowers.

And my neighbors came
to behold them,
and they said to me,
when autumn comes again,
at seeding time, will you
not give us of the seeds
of these flowers that
we may have them
in our garden?

SLEEP ABSTRACT

You are free before the sun of day,
and free before the stars of the night.
And you are free when there is
no sun and no moon and no star.
You are even free when
you close your eyes
upon all there is.

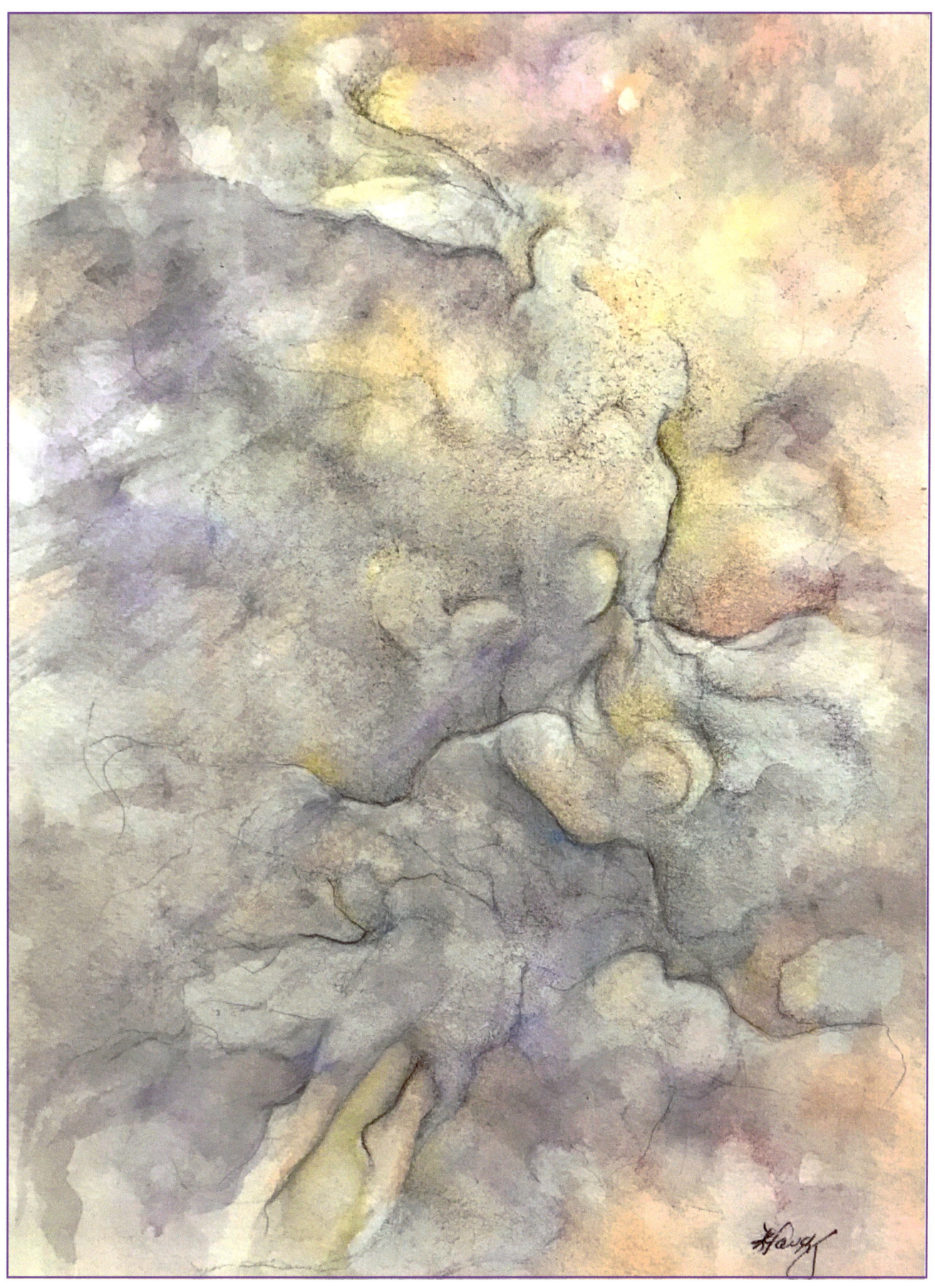

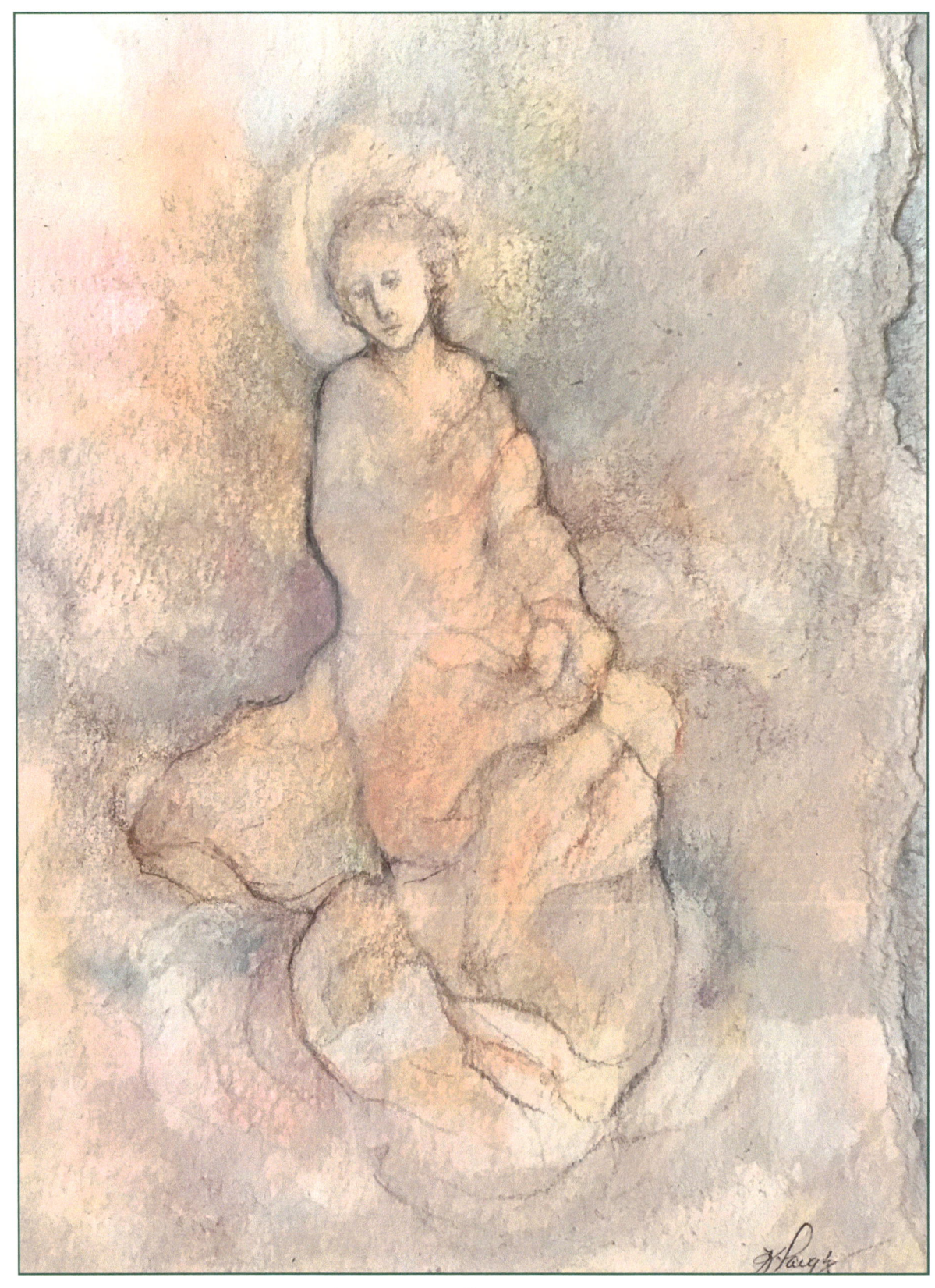

Angel of Compassion

And if you listen in the stillness of the night, you shall hear them saying in silence, Our God,
who are our winged self, it is thy will in us that wills it so.

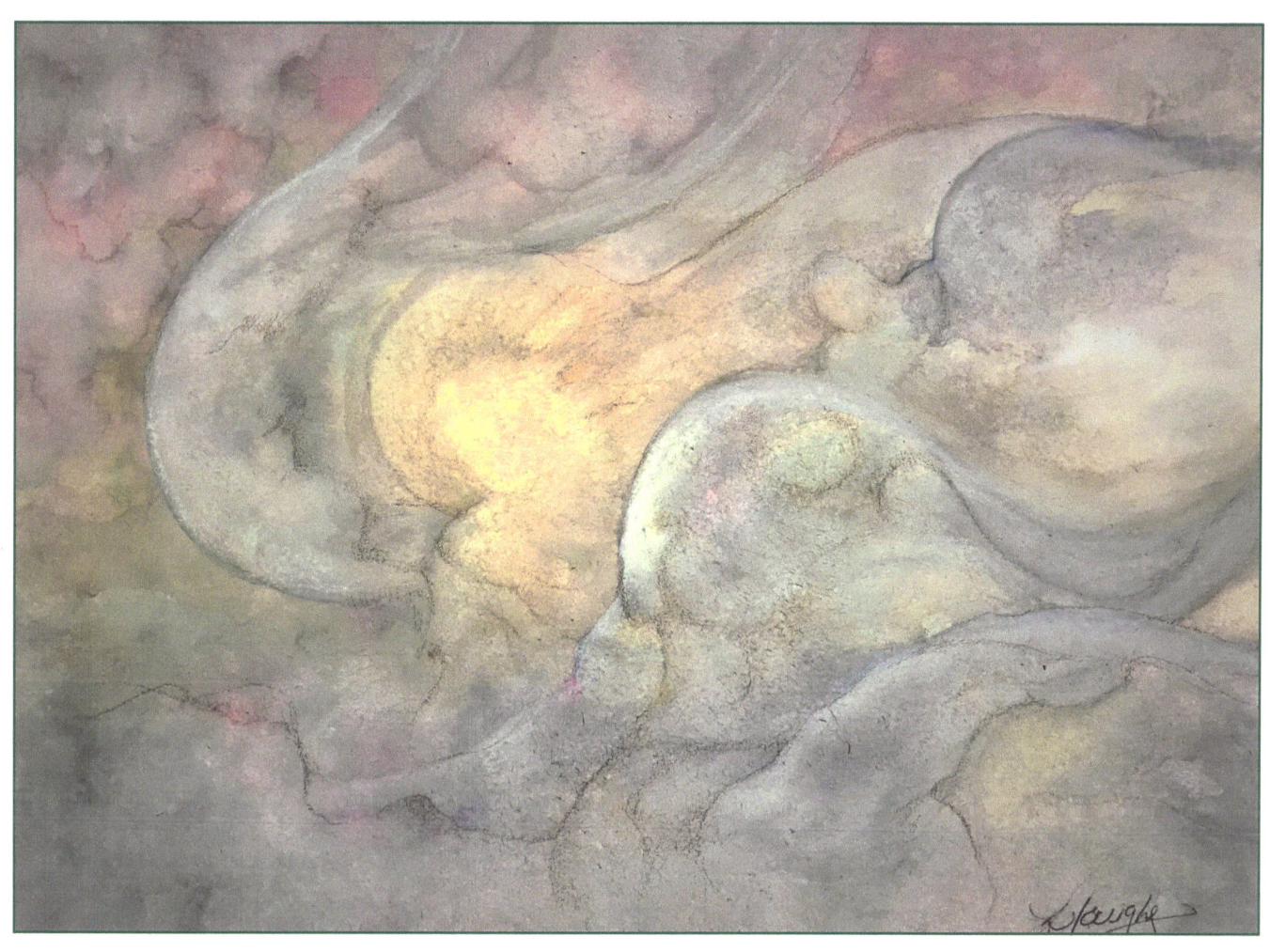

DESCENDING ANGELS

All of your hours are wings that beat through space from self to self.
He who wears his morality as his best garment were better naked.
The wind and sun will tear no holes in his skin.
And he who defines his conduct by ethics,
imprisons his song bird in a cage.

And he to whom worshiping
is a window to open and shut,
has not yet visited the house of his soul
whose windows are from dawn to dawn.

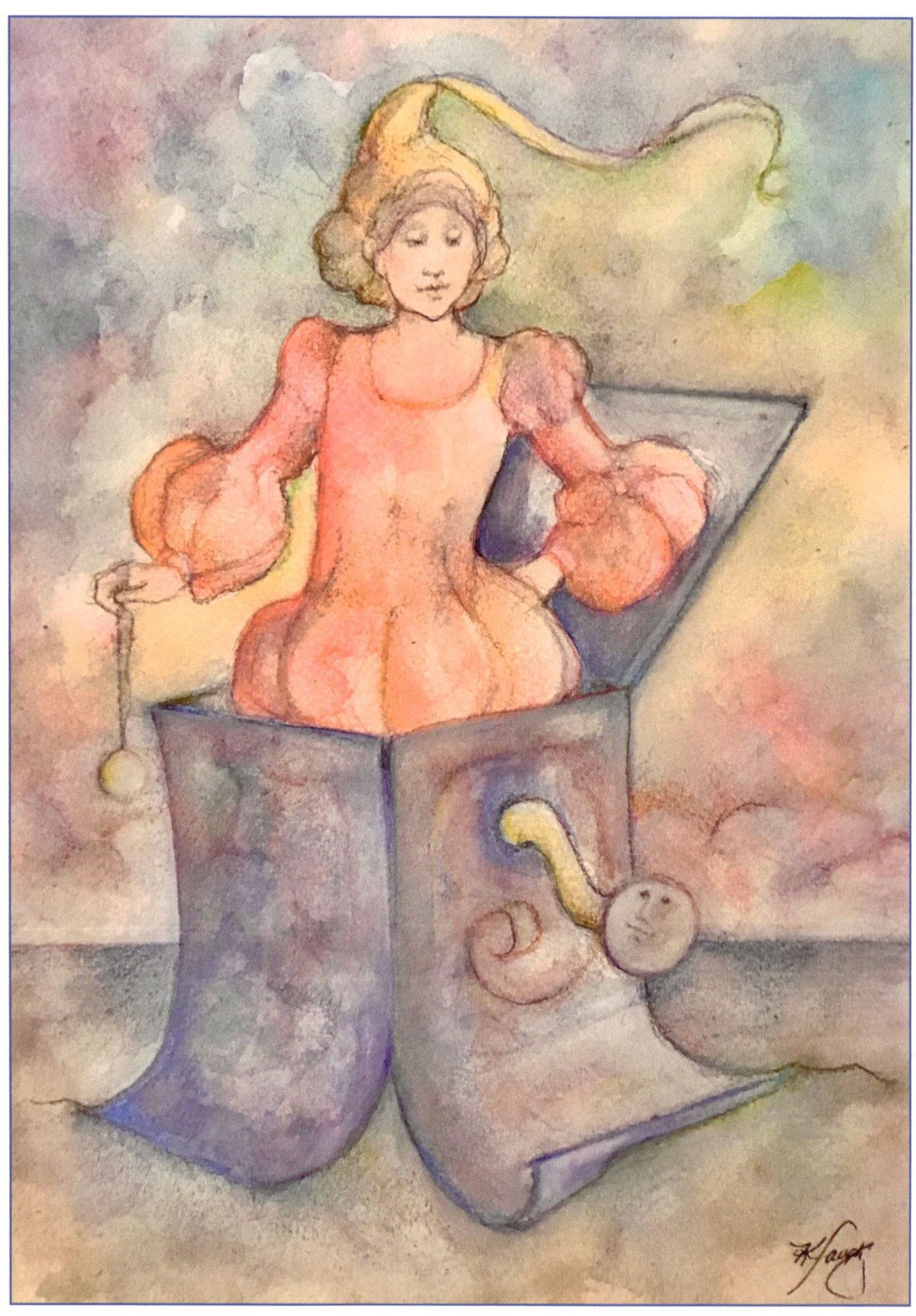

JILL IN THE BOX

Only when a juggler misses catching his ball does he appeal to me.

Only an idiot and a genius break man-made laws,
and they are the nearest to the heart of God.

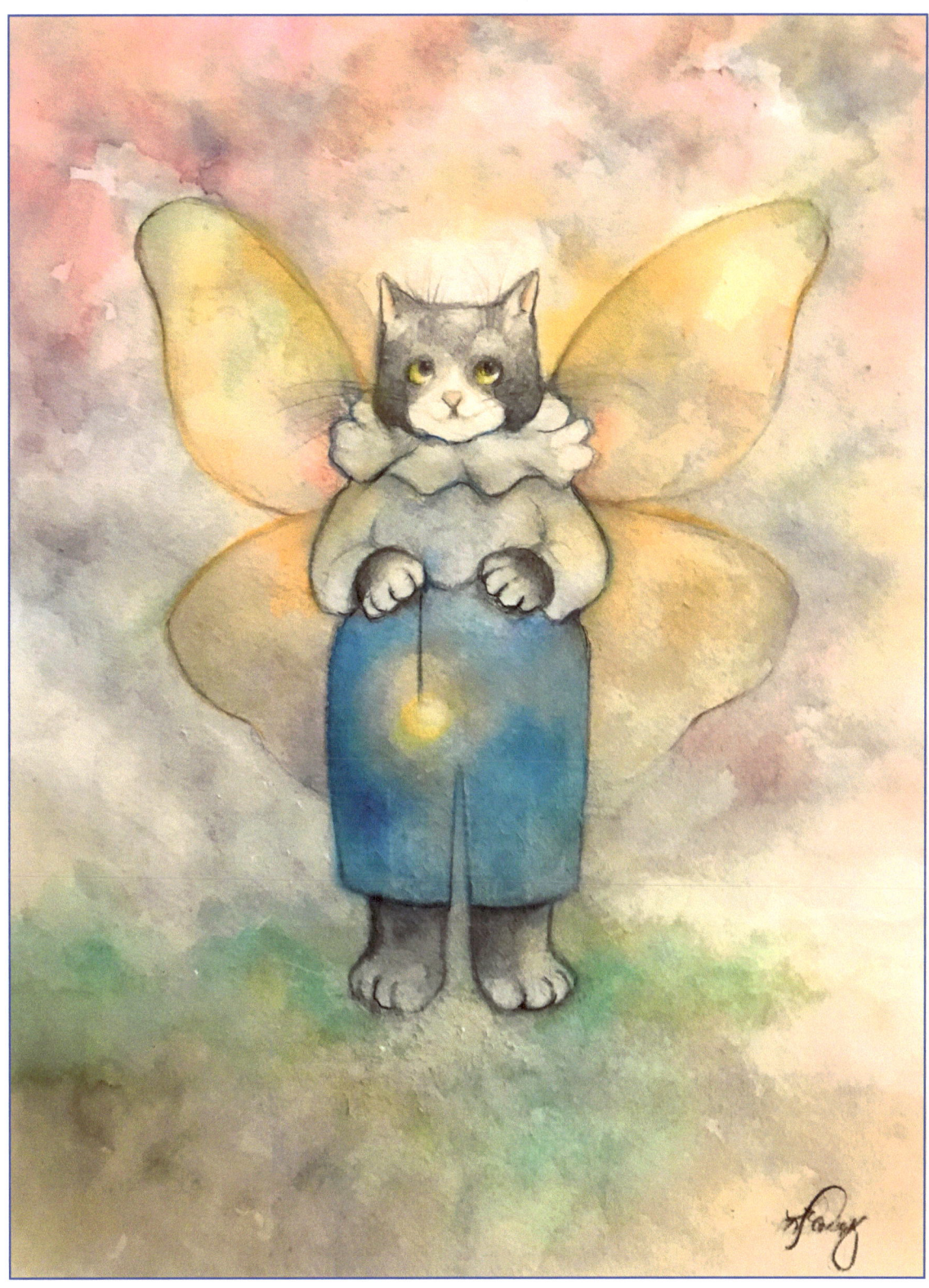

LIGHTNING BUG

The appearance of things changes according to the emotions;
and thus we see magic and beauty in them,
while the magic and beauty are really in ourselves.

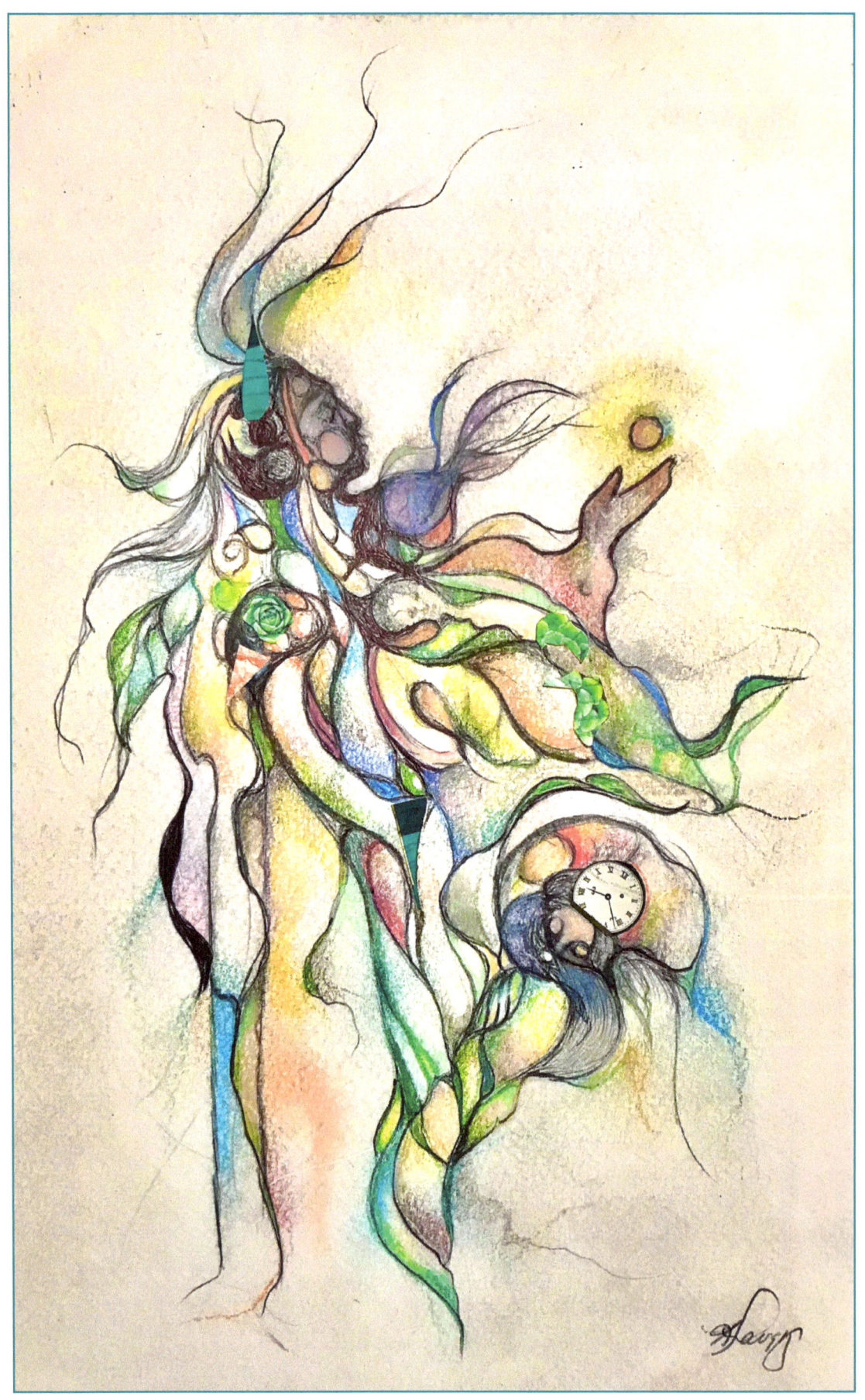

Nature Spirit

Sow a seed and the earth
will yield you a flower.
Dream your dream to the sky
and it will bring you
your beloved.
Should nature heed
what we say of contentment,
no river would seek the sea,
and no winter would
turn to spring.

Should she heed
all we say of thrift,
how many of us would
be breathing this air?

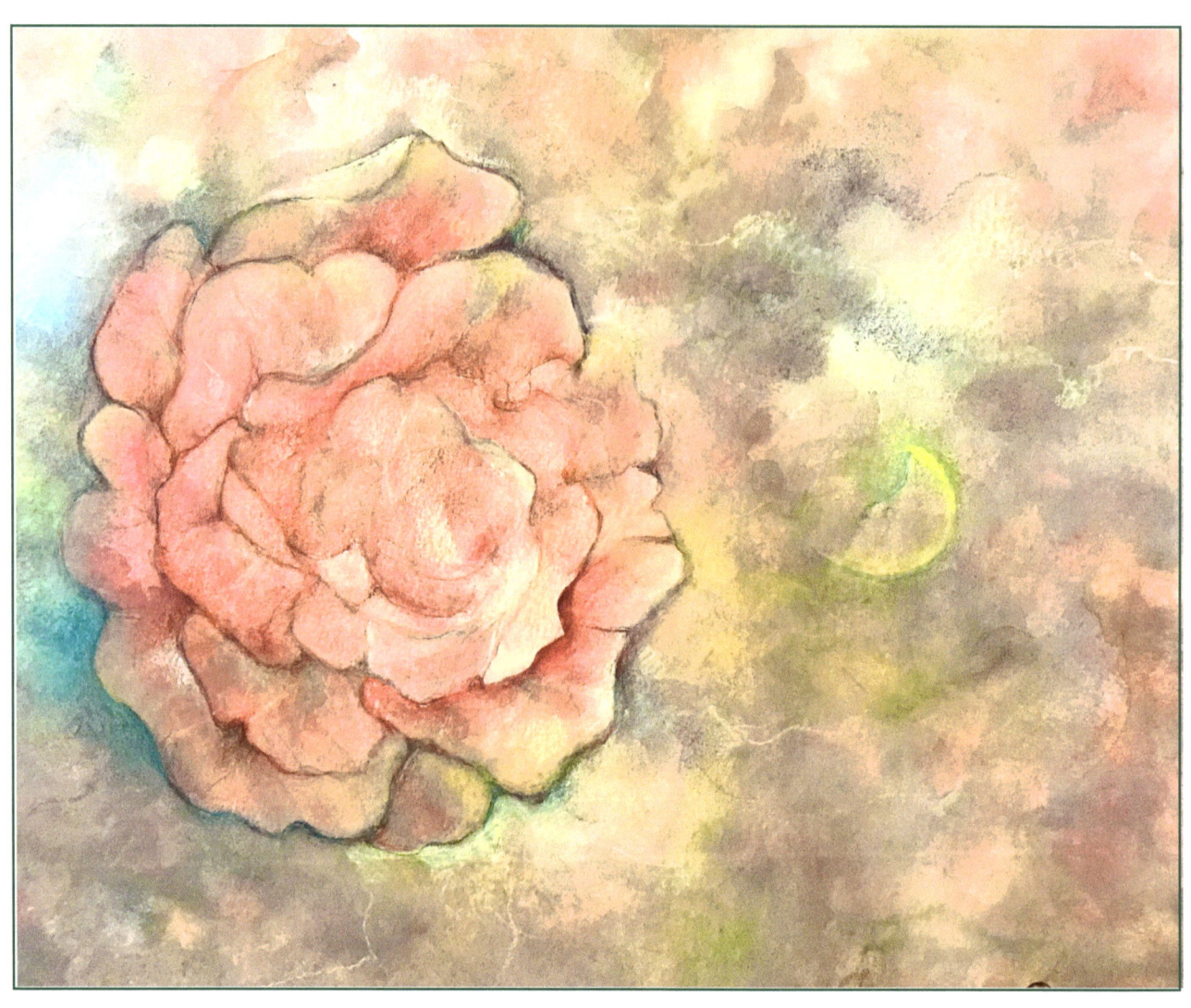

ONCE IN A BLUE MOON

The optimist sees the rose, not its thorns.

The pessimist stares at the thorns, oblivious to the rose.

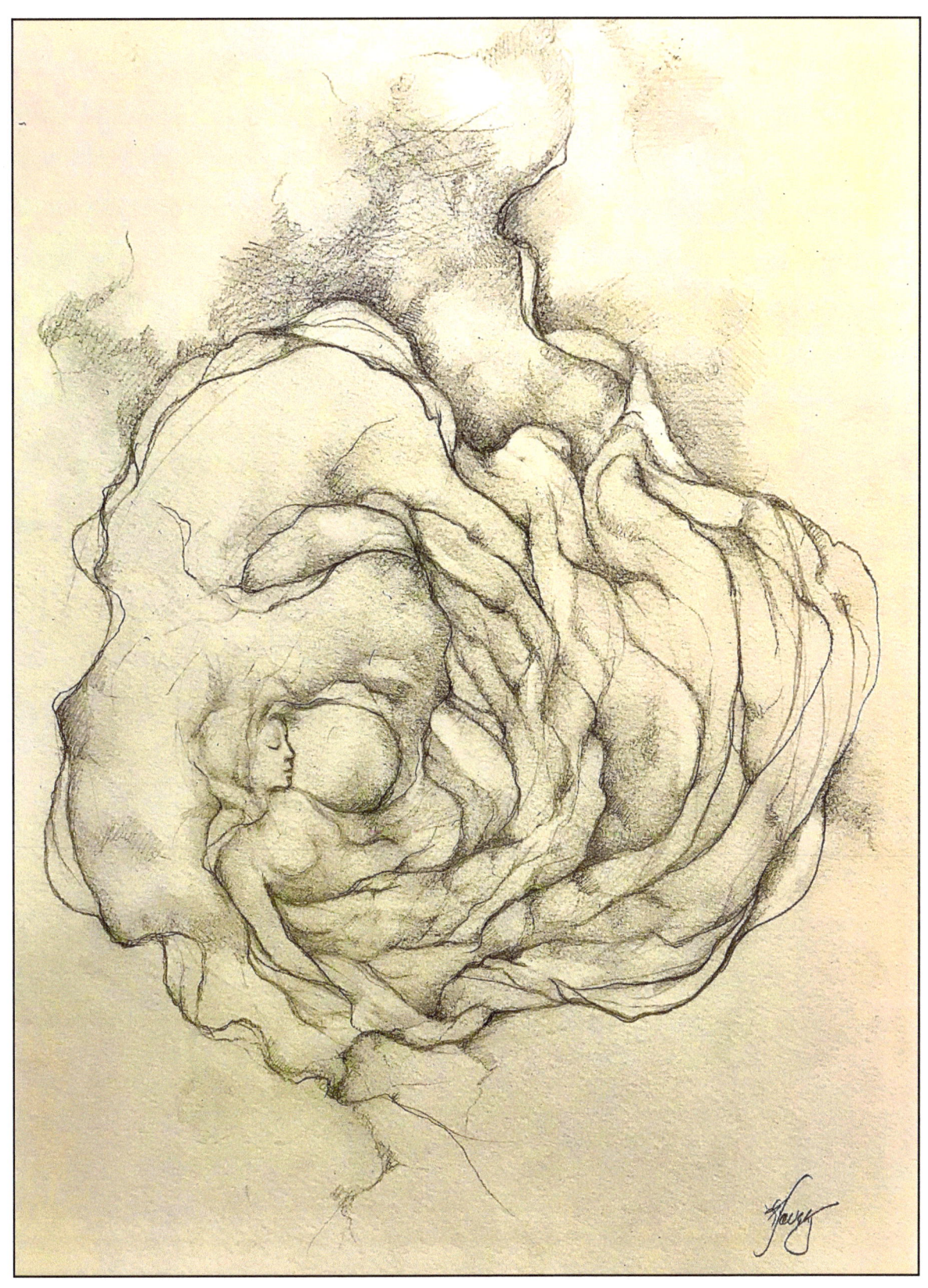

SLEEP

How can I lose faith in the justice of life when the dreams of those who sleep upon feathers are not more than the dreams of those who sleep upon the earth?

45

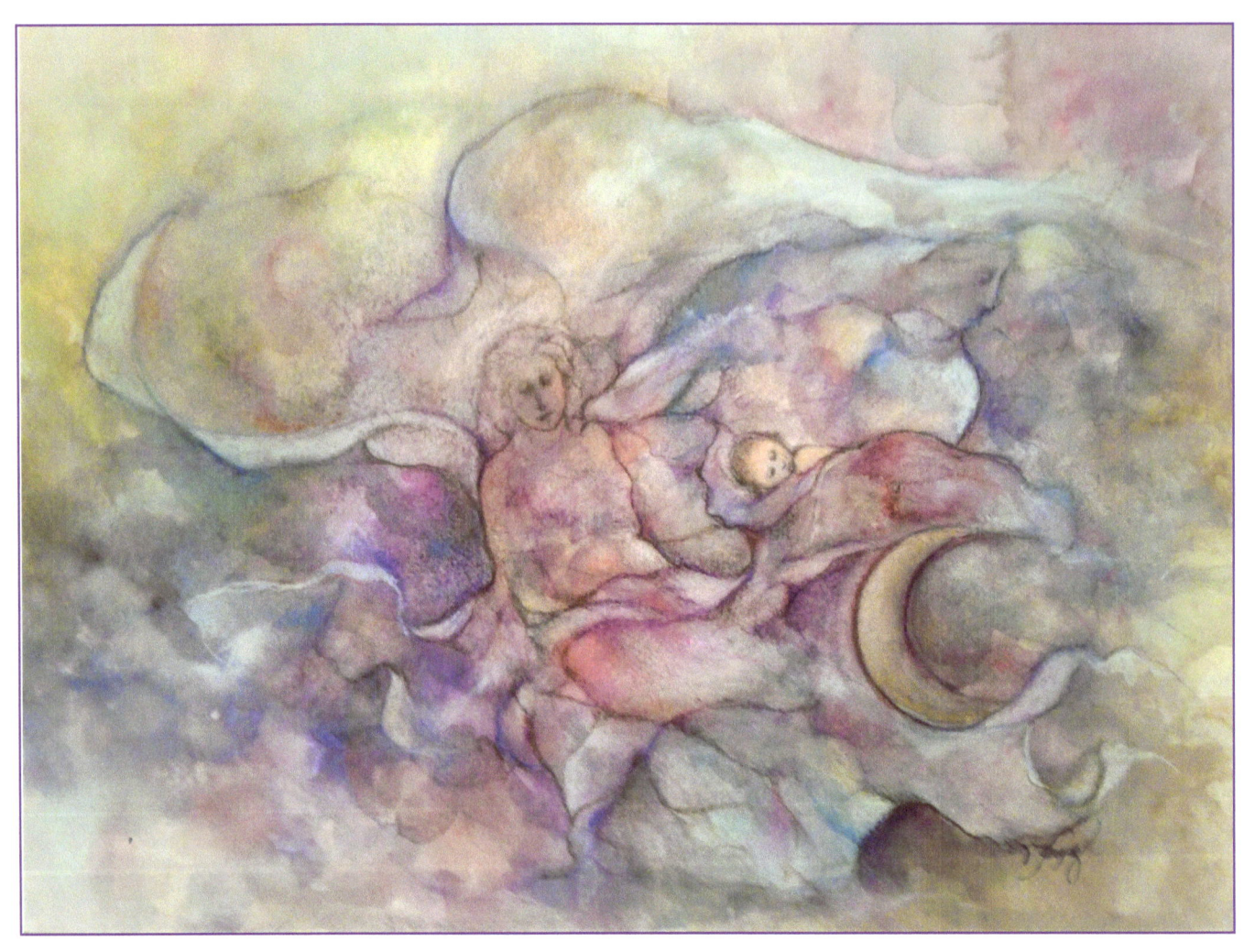

SLUMBER

We often sing lullabies
to our children that
we ourselves may sleep.

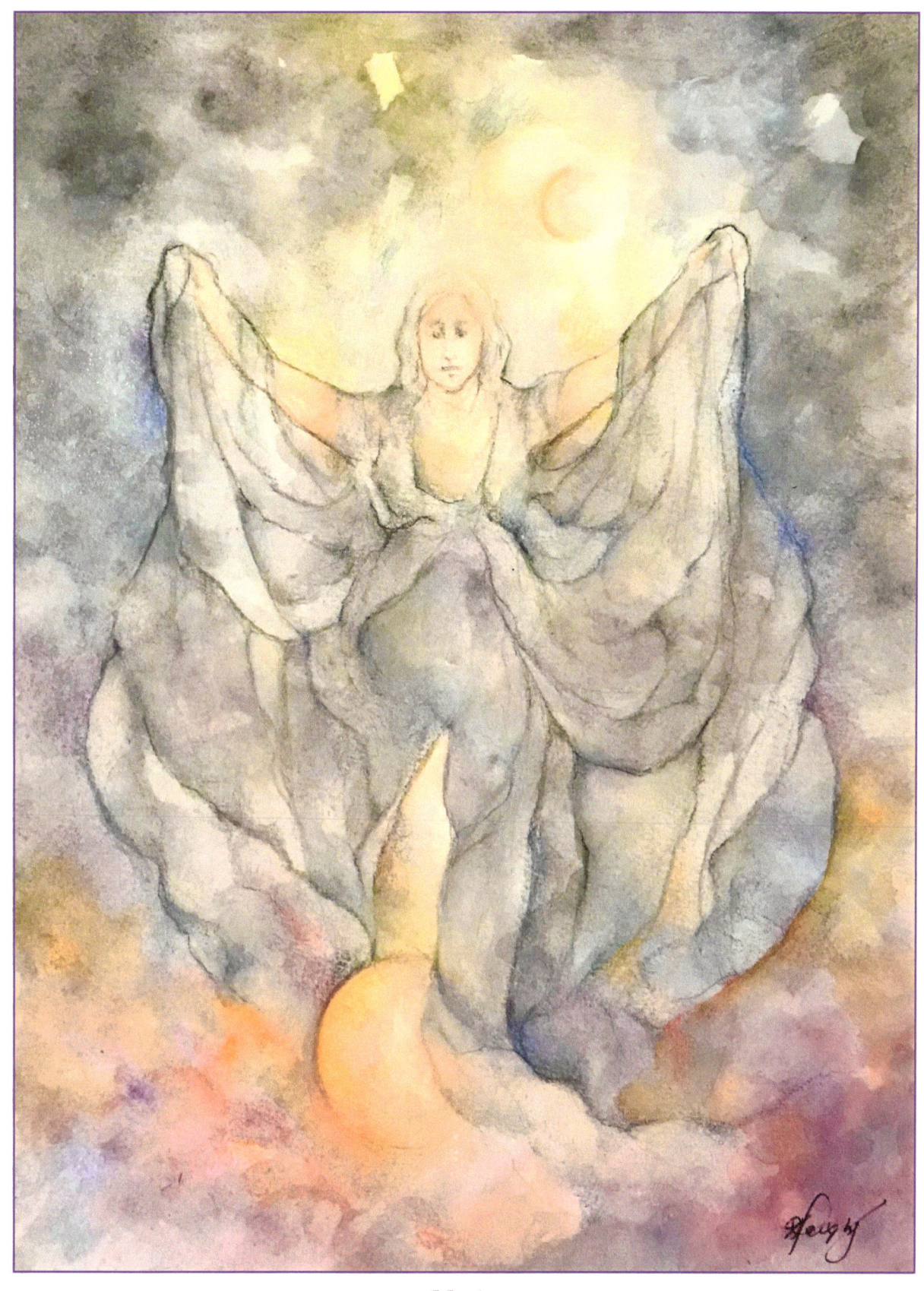

Night

Give me silence and I will out dare the night.

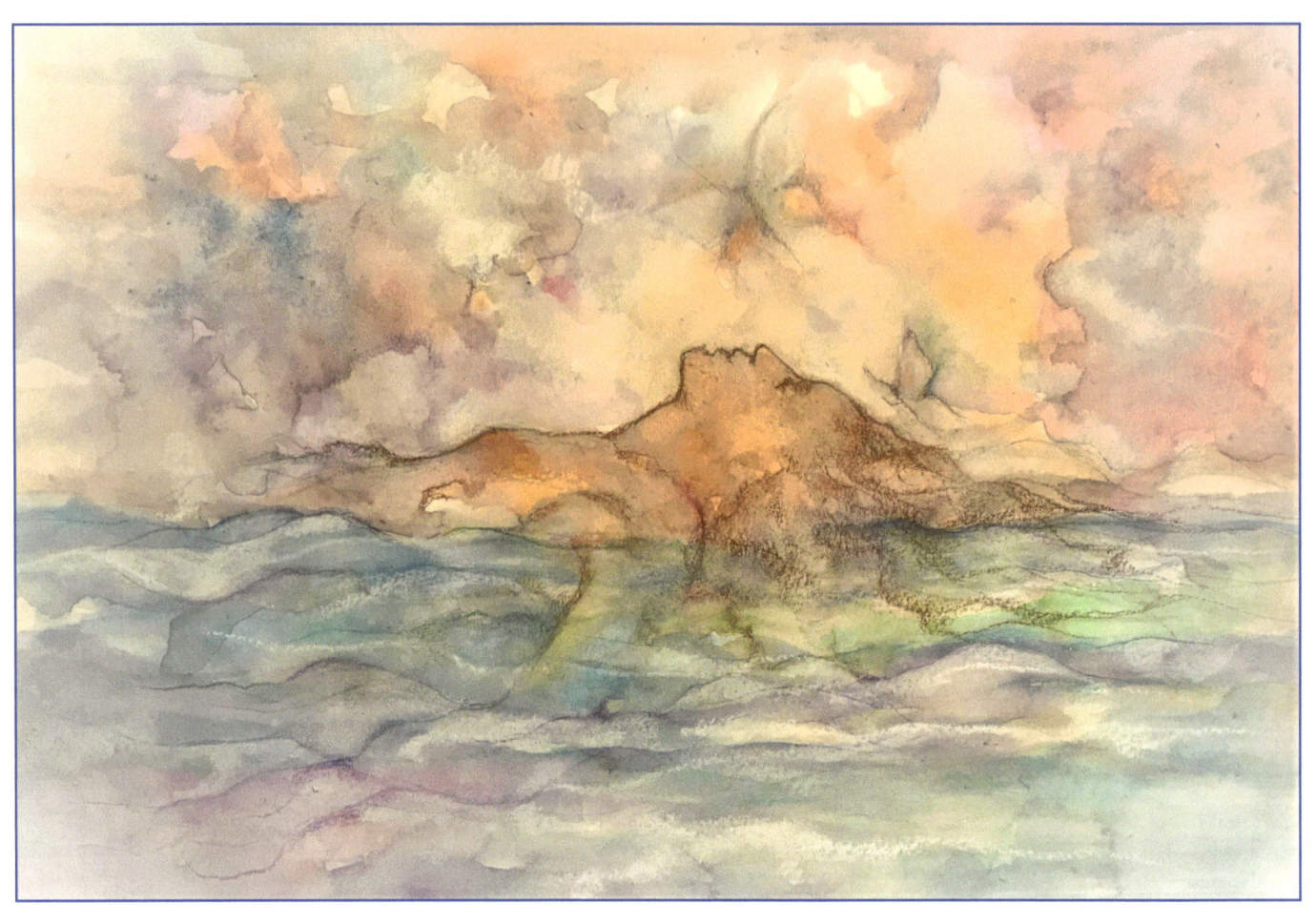

DIFFERENT WORLDS

Once I filled my hand with mist,
then I opened it,
and the mist was a worm.
And I closed and opened my hand again,
and there was a bird.
And again, I closed and opened my hand,
and its hollow stood a man
with a sad face turned upward.
And again, I closed my hand,
and when I opened it
there was naught but mist.
But I heard a song of exceeding sweetness.

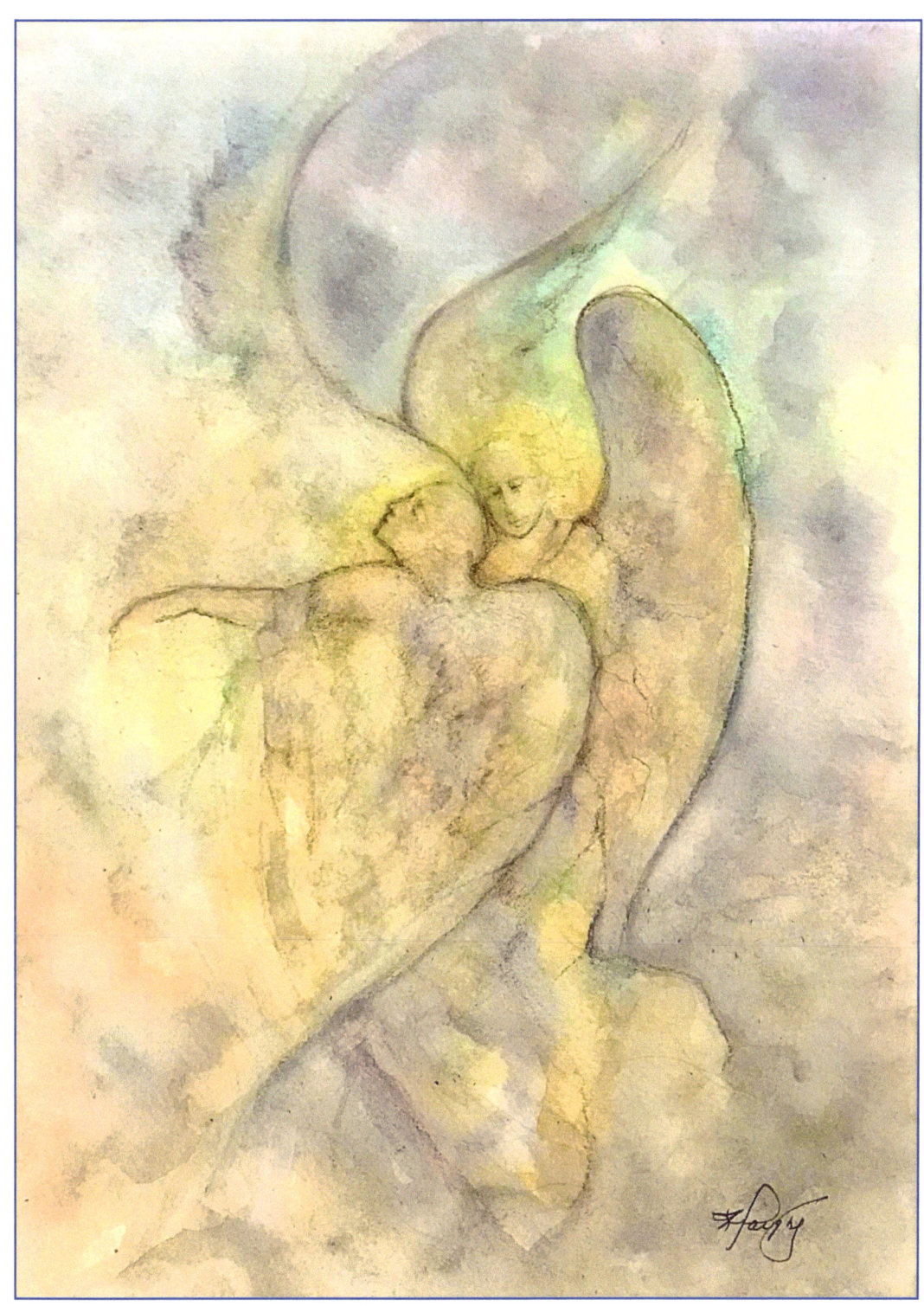

COMPASSION

And let there be no purpose in friendship save the deepening of spirit.

If he may know the ebb of your tide, let him know the flood also.

For it is his to fill your need, but not your emptiness.

For in the dew of little things, the heart finds its morning, and is refreshed.

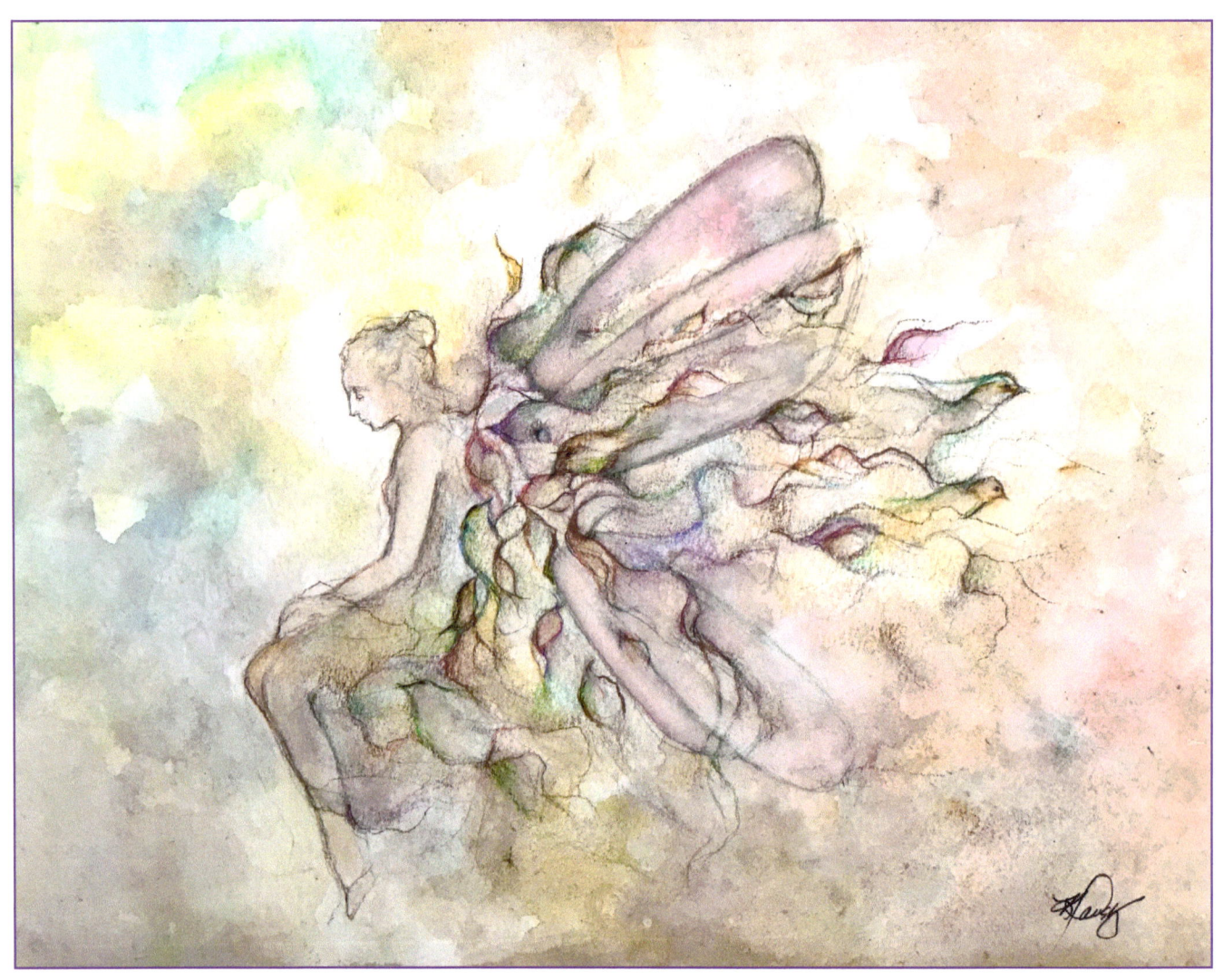

FLIGHT

Between the spiritual world and the world of substance
there is a path upon which we walk in a swoon of slumber.

It reaches us, and we are unaware of its strength.
When we return to ourselves, we find that we are
carrying with our real hands the seeds to be planted
carefully in the good earth of our daily lives,
bringing forth good deeds and words of beauty.

Were it not for that path between
our lives and the departed lives,
no prophet or poet, or learned man
would have appeared among the people.

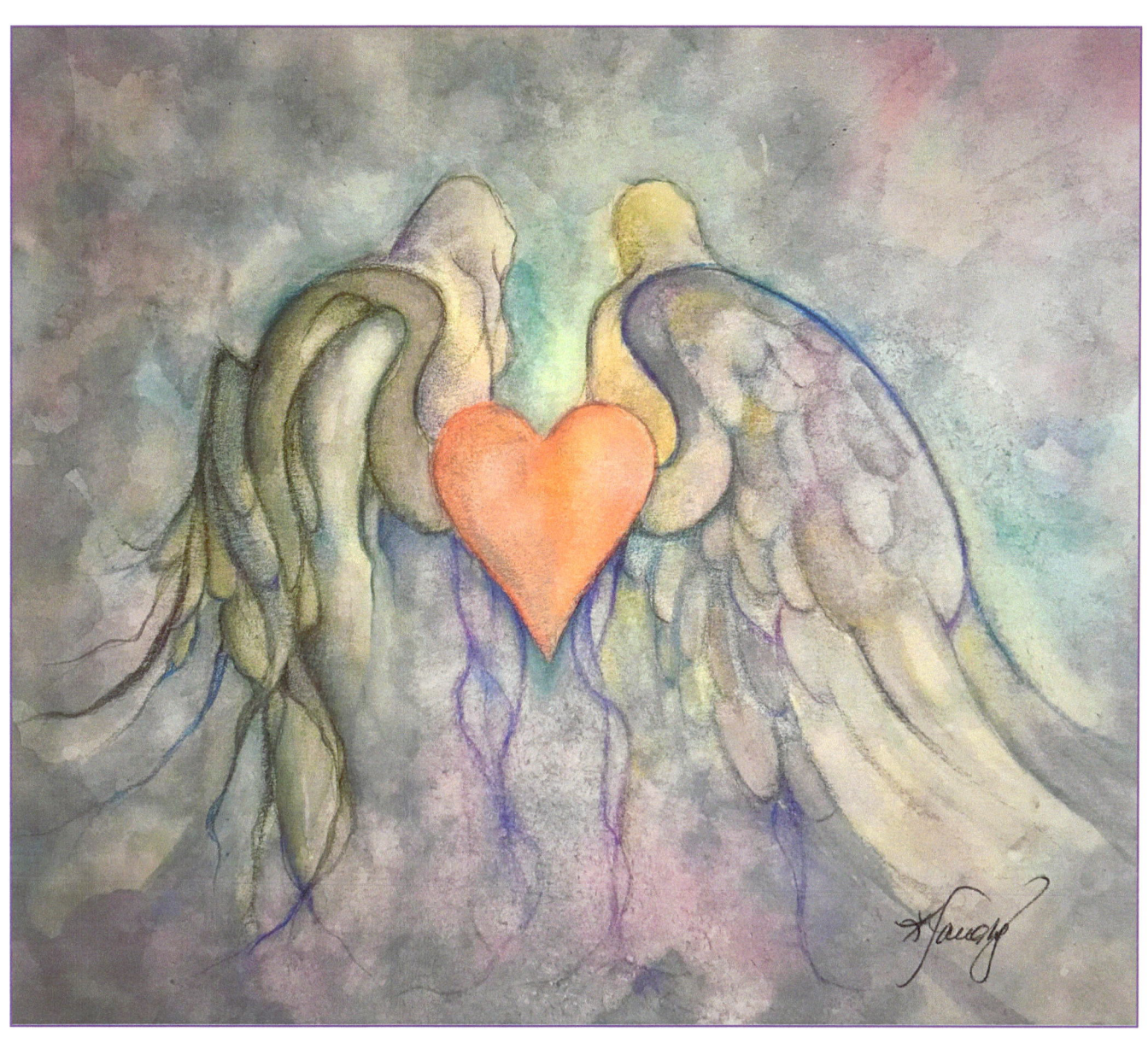

HOPE AND DESPAIR

Hope is not found in the forest,
nor the wild portray despair.
Why should the forest long
for portions when the all
is centered there?

Should one search the forest
hopeful when all nature is the aim?

For to hope is but an ailment,
so are station, wealth and fame.

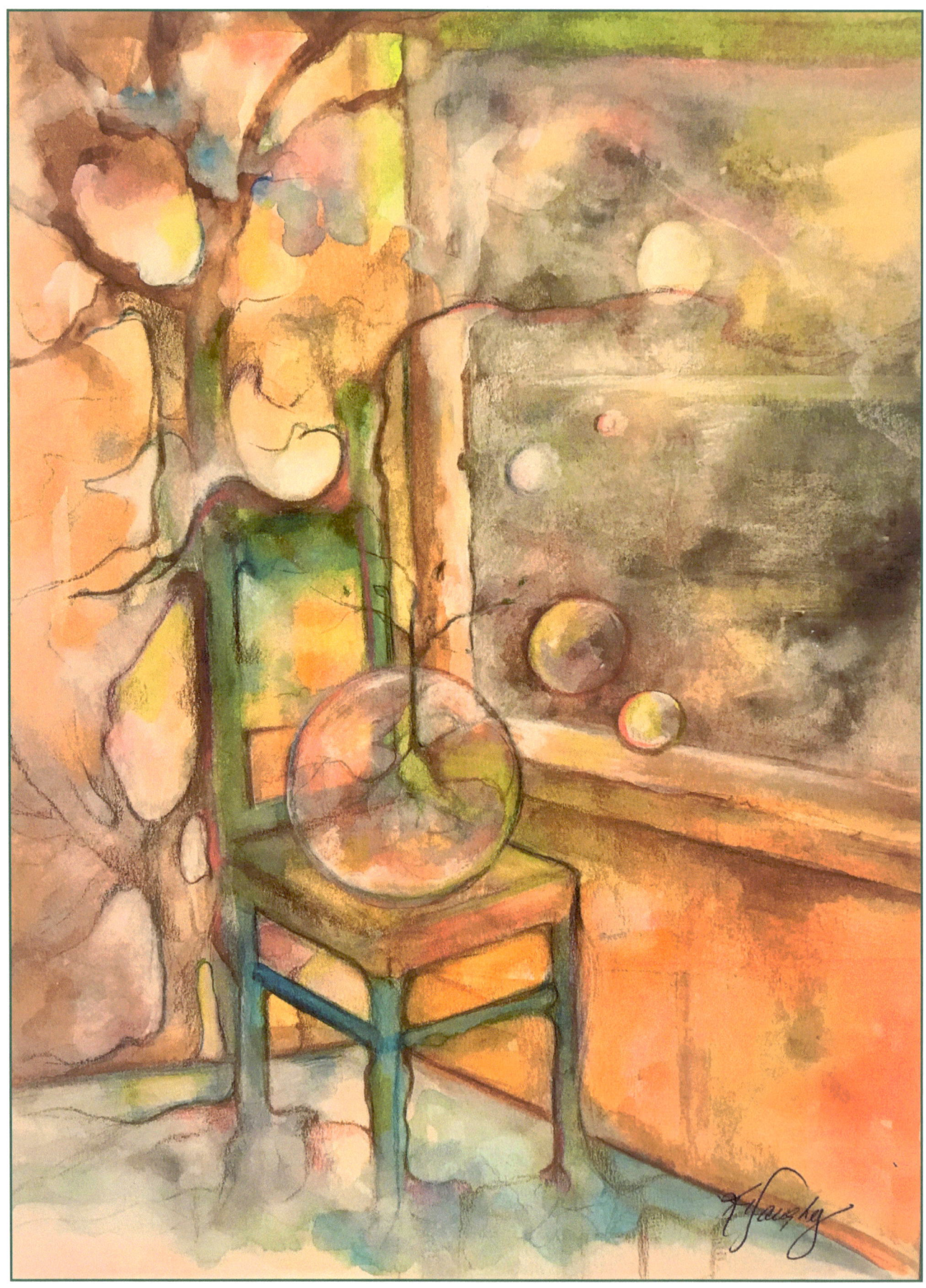

WISHING CHAIR

God has bestowed upon you
intelligence and knowledge.

Do not extinguish the lamp
of divine grace and do not let
the candle of wisdom
die out in the darkness
of lust and error.
For a wise man approaches
with his torch to light up
the path of mankind.

SEASONS

You would measure time
the measureless and
the immeasurable.

Would you then
adjust your conduct,
and even direct
the course of your spirit
according to hours and seasons?

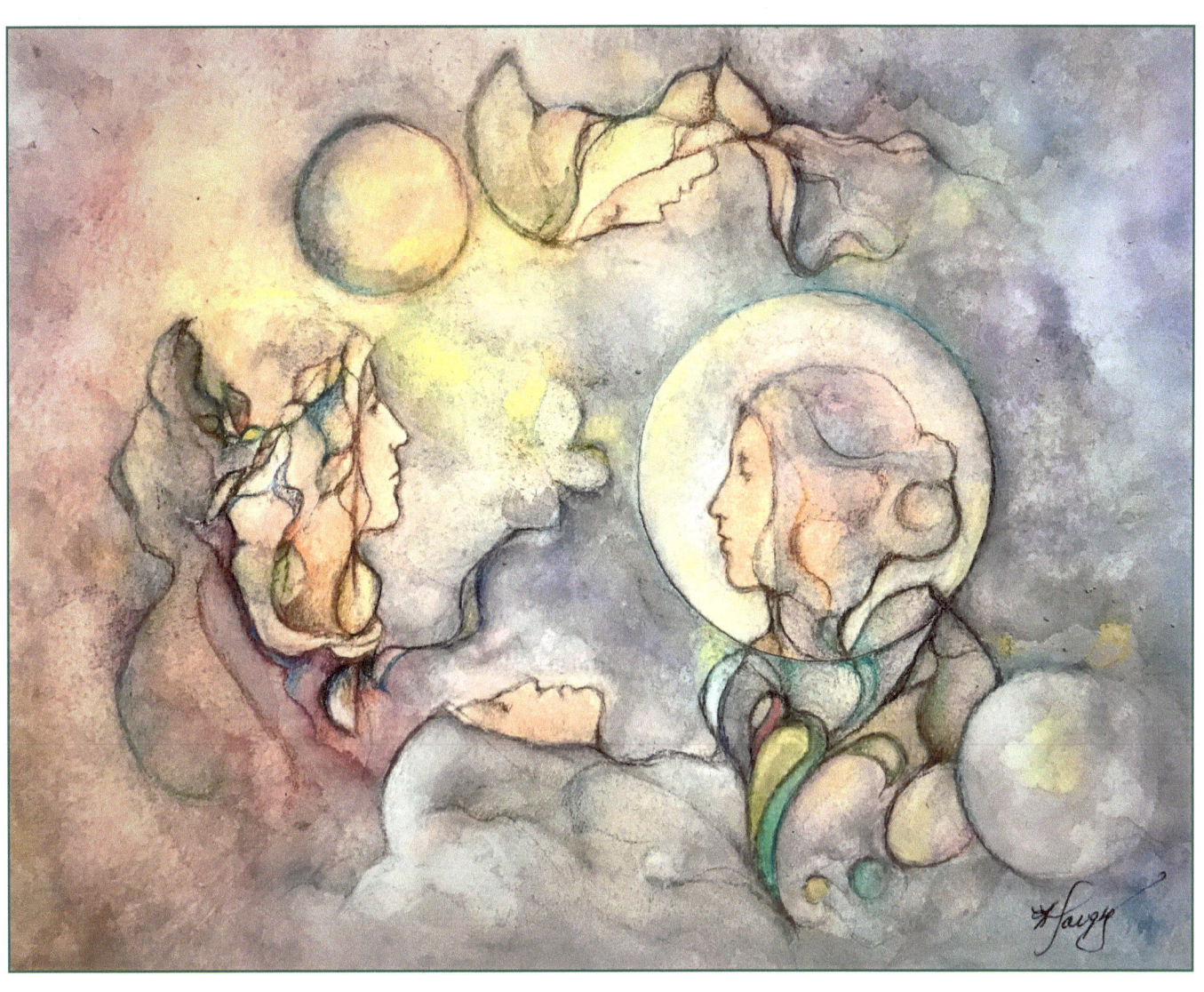

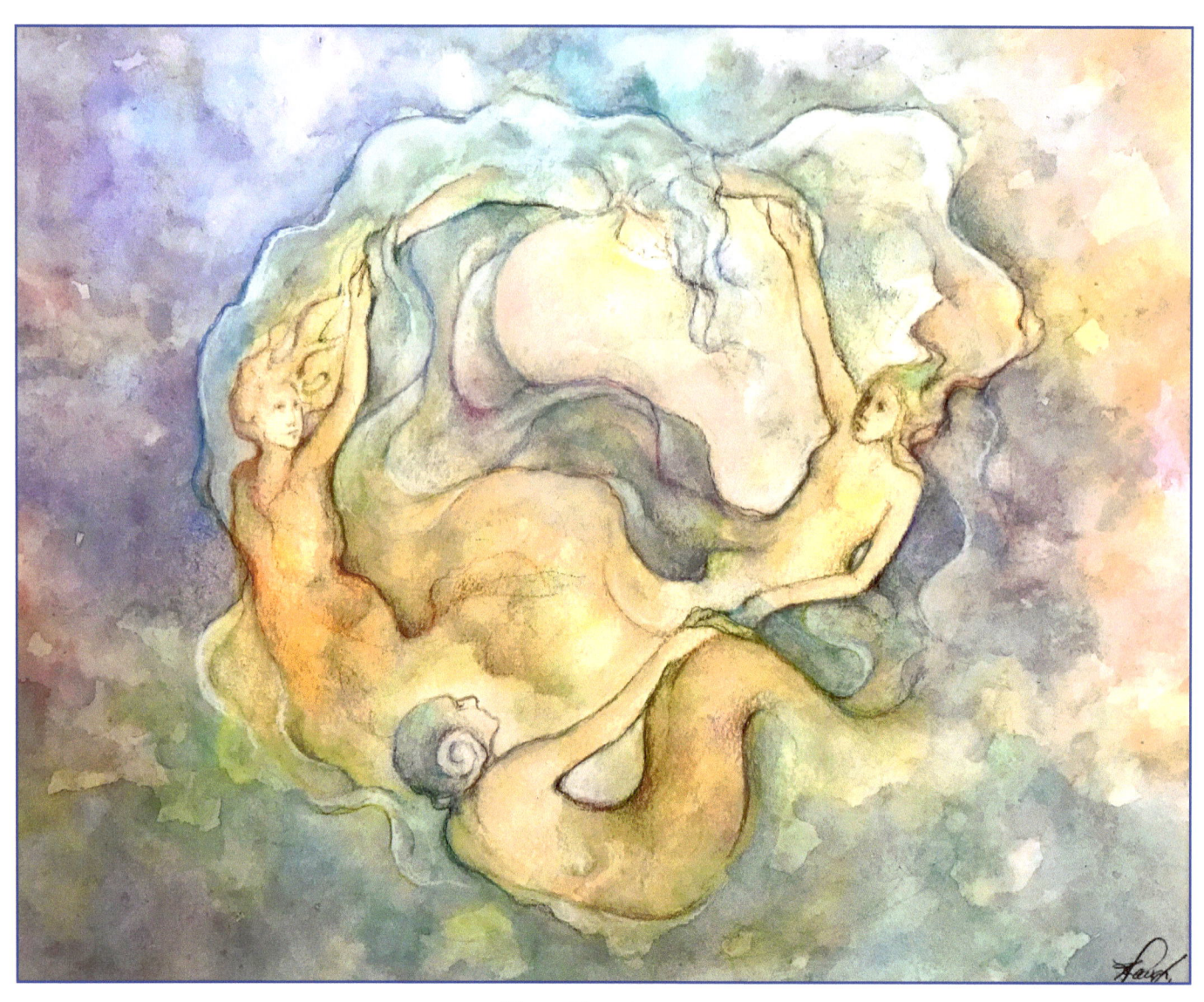

THE ELEMENTS

About the Artist

Karen M. Haughey has been an intuitive artist and author for over forty years.

Quietly observing life since early childhood, she began reading Kahlil Gibran's books, author of *The Prophet*, as early as the age of ten, as well as pursuing an interest in freehand drawing and painting.

One of his quotes in particular has always spoken clearly—
>*Art is one step from the visibly known toward the unknown.*

Deeply personal, inward visions began appearing to her in 1984 and continue to translate into etheric paintings to this day.

Her first book, *Angels, Guardians of the Light*, was published by Louise Hay in 1995, which is a culmination of ethereal art, personal philosophies, and experiences.

The original paintings contained within the book were painted in a combination of watercolor, pastel and gouache, which was not considered a typical artist technique.

Over the years she had very little professional artistic discipline or instruction, and eventually developed an unusual signature style of her own in a combination of watercolor, pastel and gouache.

She has also been an ordained, nondenominational healthcare chaplain for the past twenty-five years, serving in hospitals, and privately, throughout the San Francisco Bay Area.

She was also a former high school teacher and student advocate for Boldly Me, a national nonprofit organization that advocates wisdom, by teaching social and behavioral health, positive communication, physical wellness, and empowering self-esteem, geared toward our youth sector.

While touring nationally with Barnes and Noble and Borders Books, she also gave lectures regarding her initial spiritual experience which was also the motivating factor that led her to paint ethereal subject matter.

Since then, there have been numerous multimedia presentations regarding her life, gathered on televised interviews, You Tube lectures, and public seminars regarding Louise Hay's philosophies.

Louise Hay is the author of *You Can Heal Your Life*. Karen worked and studied with Louise personally and professionally throughout the nineties, as her art teacher and friend.

Karen's art has been shown in national galleries and in private collections from coast to coast. It has also been viewed on numerous book and magazine covers, music CD's, greeting cards, puzzle designs, which also include Andrew Ramer's book, *Angel Answers*, Gary Markowitz's *One Source, Sacred Journeys, Mindscapes*, and on the cover and contents of her latest children's book, *Rocky Gets Real* by the talented author, Cyndie Lepori. This vividly illustrated storybook is about an abandoned rocking horse that sat in a child's nursery longing to become a real horse. Wishes are real.

Most recently, she illustrated the contents and cover of the published book, *Your Celestial Guide To Exercising Healthy Choices*, written by Doctor Clare Steffen.

Karen's original artwork is now on display at Artbeat Gallery and Studio located in Sacramento, California.

She can also be found on Facebook, Instagram, LinkedIn, YouTube, and the Spiritual Connection Center's website.

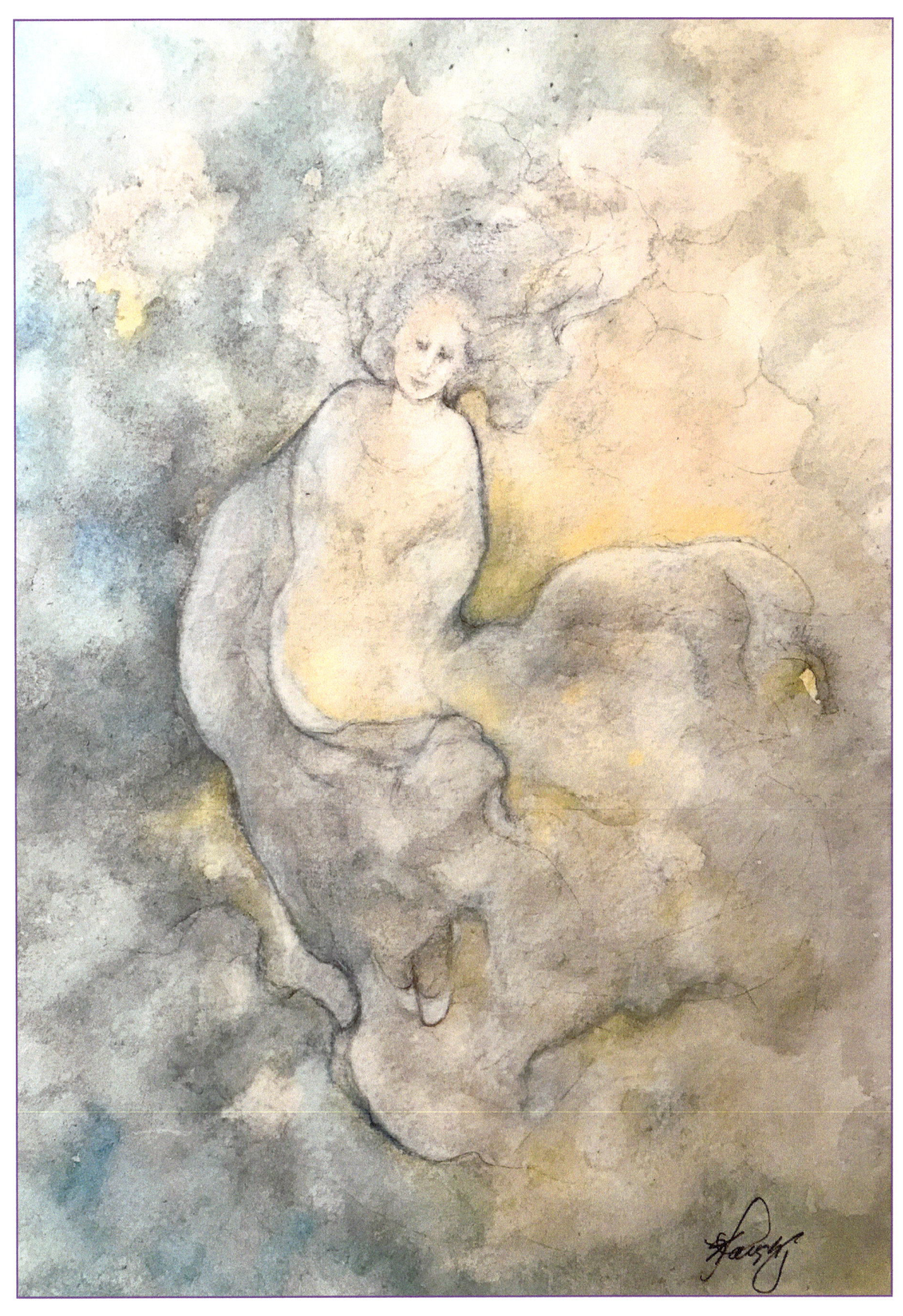

SOWING STARS

59

Also by Karen Haughey

Published Books 1995 – 2019

Angels, Guardians of the Light – Hay House, Carlsbad, California
Gratitude, Hay House – Carlsbad, California
One Source Sacred Journeys – Markowitz Publications, Honolulu, Hi.
The Angels Talk – Penguin Putman, N.Y., N.Y.
Angel Answers – Simon Schuster, N.Y., N.Y.
Mindscapes, an Artist's Thoughts and Visions – Blue Light Press

Television and Radio Broadcasts 1987 – 2003

Explorations of the Mind, Fremont, Newark, Ca.
Producer / Host / Public broadcast television.
Dateline NBC, New York, N.Y. Televised public broadcast interview.
Creative Encounters, San Jose, Ca. Televised public broadcast interview
The Gabrielle Show, Los Angeles, Ca. Televised public broadcast interview.

Selected Published Art and Articles 1987 – present

Penguin Books, N.Y., N.Y. *Angel Answers*, cover design, author, Andrew Ramer,
Angel Times Magazine, National Magazine Articles.
San Jose Mercury News, San Jose, Ca., *Argus Newspaper*, Fremont, Ca. Personal Interviews.
Master Your Mind Audio Cassette Covers/ Designs.
Spirit Art Greeting Card Co., Minneapolis, Minnesota, Greeting cards.
1996 Designer's Showcase, San Jose, Ca. Artist presentation
Fresh Start Surgical Team, San Diego, Ca. Artist presentation
Hay House, San Diego, Ca., *Angels, Guardians of the Light*. International book publication.
Realizing Potentials Publications, New Mexico, *Angelic Awakenings*,
author, Jessica Eccles, Book cover design.
World Disc Productions, San Juan Island, Washington. Peter Sterling's C.D Covers.
Dream, Electric Angels, Fremont, Ca., C.D. Cover Designs.
ARC, San Diego, Ca., Book Cover and Material Designs.
Connections Puzzles, Honolulu, Hi. Art / Designs for puzzles.
Tri City Voice newspaper, Fremont, Ca. Interview